T0271636

accessories

THE HOME EDIT™

stay organized

The Ultimate Guide to
MAKING SYSTEMS STICK

CLEA SHEARER & JOANNA TEPLIN

MITCHELL BEAZLEY

THE INTELLIGENT INVESTOR
The Banker's WIFE
auto 110
DAN BROWN ANGELS & DEMONS
NEW YORK FASHION
YES WE (STILL) CAN DAN PFEIFFER
How to Cook Everything
TOM WOLFE I AM CHARLOTTE SIMMONS
DENNIS McNALLY
DARING GREATLY
MOLLY SIMS
THE LAST MRS PARRISH
We Are Water
DAN BROWN ORIGIN
domino
PULL UP A CHAIR
Valley of the Dolls

To the people who think they will
never get organized or stay organized.
This one is for you.

La Croix
bubly
sparkling water
blueberry pomegranate
WATERLOO
GRAPE
Sabra Snackers
Palmetto Cheese
Original
Lowfat Cottage Cheese
Small Curd
Moisture Fresh Crisper / Bac Humidit
Moisture Fresh Crisper / Bac Humidit

Contents

cricut
cricut
cameras
cameras

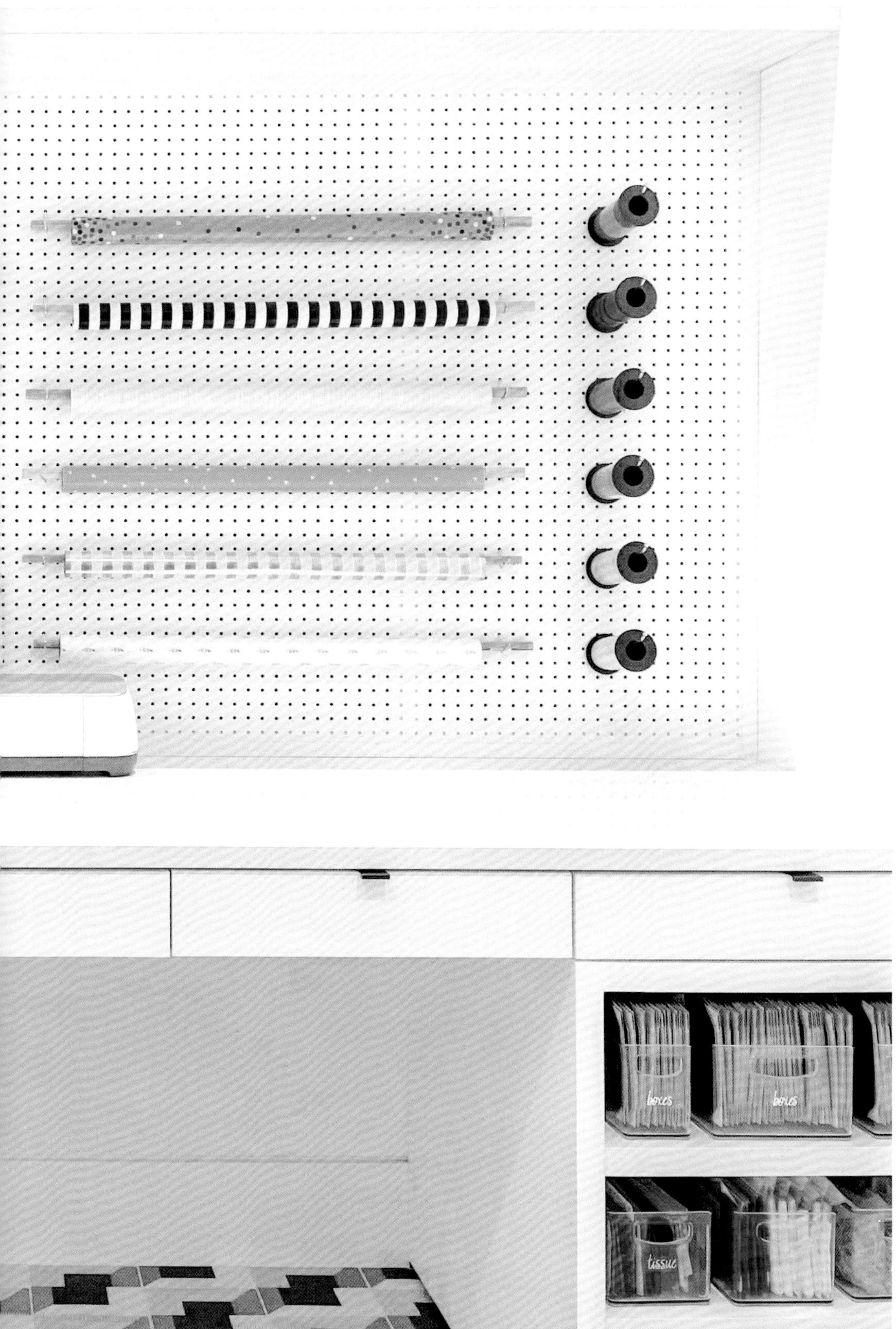
boxes
boxes
tissue

Introduction

Raise your hand if you've ever filled an entire shopping cart with clear bins, turntables, and sets of canisters in each size, expecting them to transform your life overnight, but the items *still* ended up where they didn't belong.

Or if you've scrolled through our Instagram feed, taking screenshots of pantries and closets with items perfectly arranged in rainbow order, having every intention to re-create the look at home, only for those images to become buried deep within your camera roll because you think, "Why put in all that effort if my kids are just going to mess it up?"

Which could be why you decided to pick up this book in the first place. You want to be organized but can't seem to get there or stay there. Here's the truth: If you want your systems to stick, you have to make organizing a lifestyle. Embracing that reality is the only answer.

But don't worry. We're not here to make you feel guilty, lazy, or bad about yourself. Rather, we're here to help you get back on track and be your biggest cheerleaders. (Just don't be alarmed if one of us attempts a toe touch at some point.)

Do our homes ever get messy? Yes, of course they do! Every house gets messy, particularly when you add spouses, children, and pets—i.e., any living, breathing creature who is not you. But what we are quick to tell people is that, while our houses get messy, they never get disorganized . . . and that's something different. Once you have smart systems that can flex over time, it's not hard to stay on track.

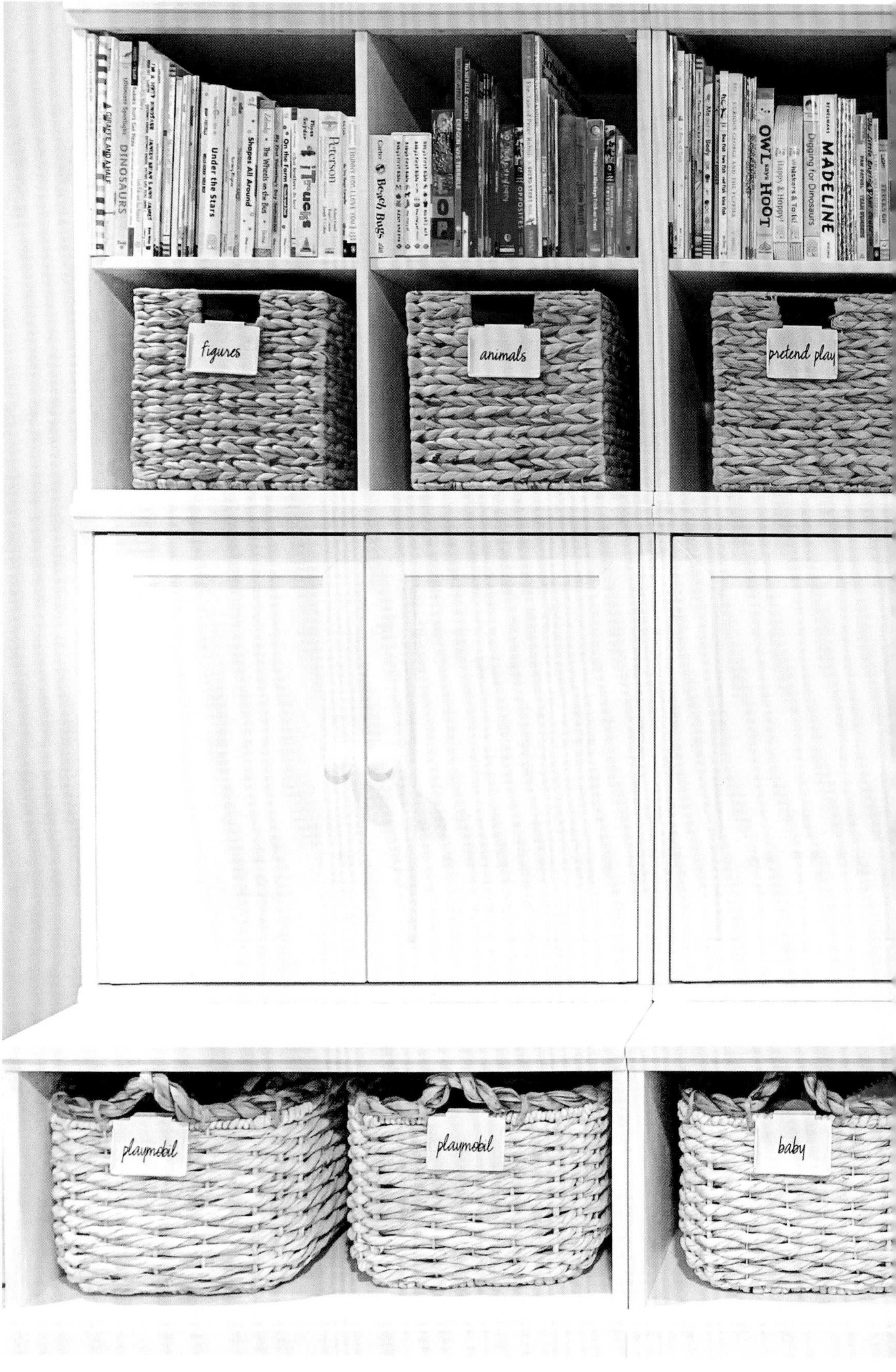

figures
animals
pretend play
playmobil
playmobil
baby
Under the Stars
MADELINE
Digging for Dinosaurs
OWL says HOOT
DINOSAURS

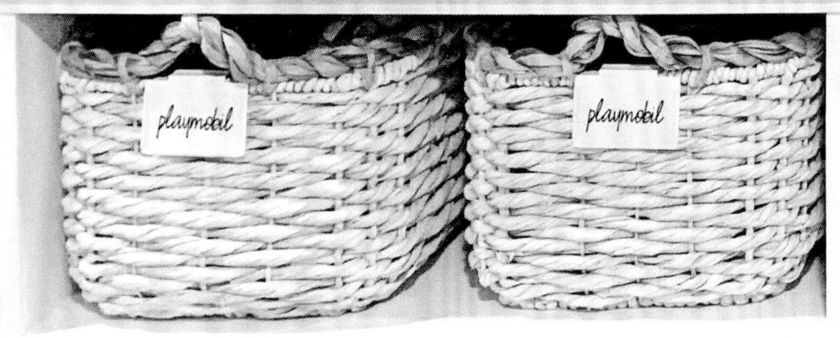

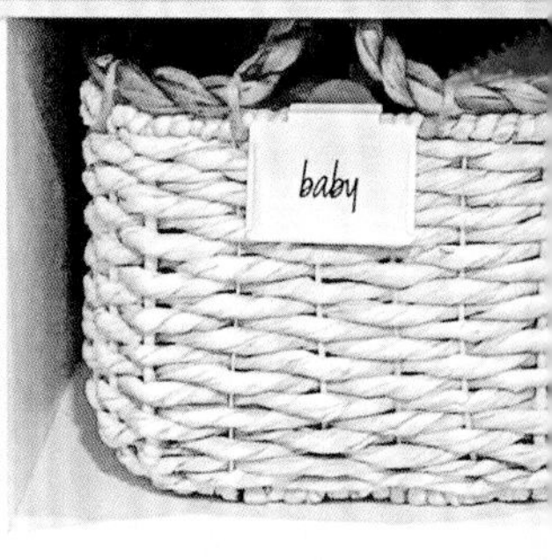

pop-up peekaboo
Dinoshapes
The EASTER EGG
PAW Patrol 5-Minute Stories
SUPER HERO BEDTIME STORIES
WAITING IS NOT EASY!
MOTHER GOOSE TREASURY
My Best Pet
NOISY BABY ANIMALS
TOUCH EXPLORE
ABC WHAT CAN SHE BE?
Under the Sea
Pop up Garden
building
building
building
baby
music
music

Maintenance is not one and done. We have found over the years that people are . . . not totally in love with that reality. Sure, it's tempting to set up a system and forget it, but hello? Do you live in a museum? Maintenance is the answer to organizing, and the thought of staying organized is what impedes many people from getting organized in the first place. And we promise you it's not as hard or scary as you think it is!

SO, LET'S TALK ABOUT HOW TO USE THIS BOOK.

The chapters that follow will take you through the spaces in your house, on a journey from what is typically the easiest spot (the entry) to the most challenging (the garage). You might already know how much we love a gold star, so we've given the entry a 1-gold-star rating and the garage a 9-star rating. (We wanted to give the garage 25 stars because that's how much we dislike organizing the garage, but we're nothing if not consistent.) As you use this book, are we suggesting you reward yourself with the appropriate number of stars after you revive each space? Oh, 100 percent.

- **What this book is:** a user-friendly guide, divided by room, complete with checklists and scripts to help you stay organized once you already did the work of getting organized. If you haven't started organizing yet, this book will get you there.

- **What this book isn't:** a report card. No one will be graded here! If you've been on this wild ride with us long enough, you know that we are very good at exactly one thing. Organizing. Don't ask us to craft, or cook you dinner, or go outside and play catch. No, like seriously . . . you'd quickly regret it. And just as we can't tell you the square root of 9 (no matter how many times you repeat the question, or even explain the concept), we don't expect you to look at a space and immediately know how you've gone off the rails. Leave that part to the experts. Us! If you try not to judge us about the math thing, we promise not to judge your closets. Deal? Deal.

If you use this book as intended, you will end up with systems that stick for every room. And if (more like when) things start to slip, pick this book back up again. Or skip to the end of each chapter, where we give you Low-Bar Lifestyle Long-Term Goals, aka your future-focused reality check. Because life is messy. But if you're honest with yourself and are willing to do just a little bit every day, it never needs to get disorganized.

SCENTIVA
Tumble
method
Cascade
Snuggle
Lysol
5 PC LAUNDRY EDIT
2 X EVERYTHING: STACKING BIN
1 X THE TURNTABLE
2 X EVERYTHING: NARROW BIN
THE HOME EDIT

STAR RATING SYSTEM

★☆☆☆☆☆☆☆☆ **One Star:** Entry

★★☆☆☆☆☆☆☆ **Two Stars:** Laundry/Utility

★★★☆☆☆☆☆☆ **Three Stars:** Bathroom

★★★★☆☆☆☆☆ **Four Stars:** Kids' Zones

★★★★★☆☆☆☆ **Five Stars:** Home Office

★★★★★★☆☆☆ **Six Stars:** Closet

★★★★★★★☆☆ **Seven Stars:** Kitchen

★★★★★★★★☆ **Eight Stars:** Pantry/Fridge

★★★★★★★★★ **Nine Stars:** Garage

SYSTEM VS. MAINTENANCE

Let's get this clear from the beginning: Is this a book about maintenance, or is this a book about setting up the right systems?

IT'S ABOUT BOTH!!

You see, those two things—having the right systems and maintaining them—are inextricably linked. We sometimes hear from people who spent precious time creating a system that didn't work for them. They are frustrated, disappointed, and ultimately take all the blame. But then we start asking questions. There's always more to the story as to why they can't devote as much time and energy to maintenance as they once did.

But does that mean all maintenance? Of course not! The last place we want you to end up is in the "If I can't maintain this, I can't maintain anything" trap. If you have a system that's gone off the rails a bit, maybe you didn't ask yourself enough questions before you started. It could be as simple as that. Or maybe your life has really changed, in a big way (new house, new baby, new hobby that requires a lot of bulky equipment—like Seth Rogen taking up pottery . . . he needs to call us). In other words, the space isn't your problem—it's your lifestyle around the space.

As much as we'd love to teleport ourselves into your living room for an impromptu question and answer sesh, we're a ways off from that technology being invented. So, you're going to have to follow the guidance in this book with a healthy sense of self-knowledge. Think not about how you'd like to live, but how you already do live (if you love the look of clear pantry bins but are never going to decant your cereal, there are other methods that will work better for you). Ditto for the members of your family (if your kids take their shoes off right by the door but you put the shoe storage in the hall closet, you're setting yourself up for failure). You know what they say: To know thyself is the beginning of wisdom, and it keeps you from having a pantry that stresses you over spice storage.

A Completely Unscientific, In-No-Particular-Order

LIST OF WHY MAINTENANCE CAN FEEL IMPOSSIBLE

- Wrong-for-you system
- Lack of time
- Family members not getting on board
- Old habits dying hard
- Household having too many things
- Unrealistic expectations

And these are all insurmountable. **Let's review the organizing basics:**

Step 1: Edit. Pare down by tossing or donating items you don't love, need, or have a sentimental connection to.

Step 2: Categorize. Group like items together in a way that makes sense for how they're used in your life.

Step 3: Contain. Give items a designated home with organizing tools, or what we call "product" (bins, baskets, turntables, shelves, drawers, etc.).

Step 4: Maintain. Regularly.

chocolate collagen
chocolate protein
strawberry protein
vanilla protein
vanilla protein
collagen

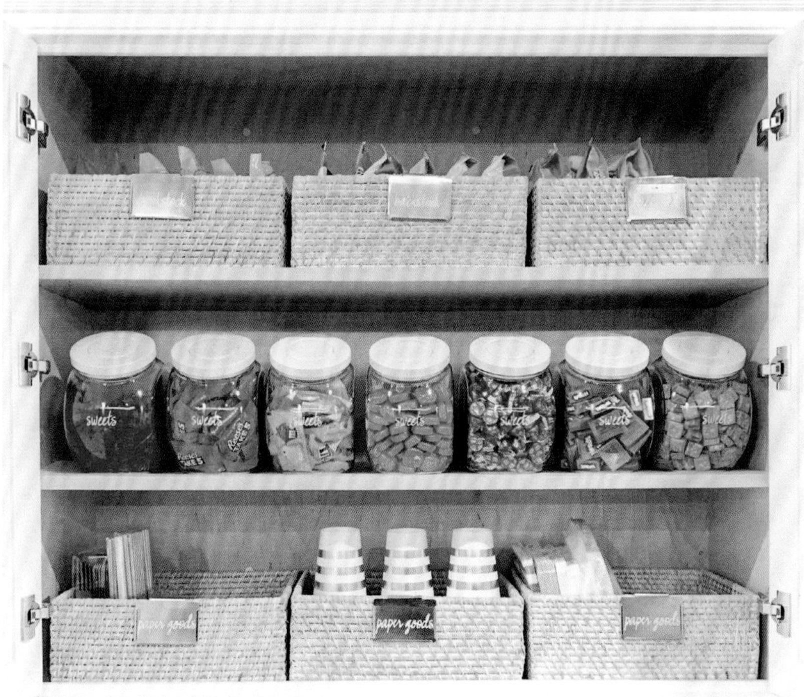

BACKSTOCK IS EVERYTHING

We've said it before, and we'll say it again: Being organized doesn't mean you must inherently own fewer things. It just means you need to be thoughtful about what you do own so you can accommodate for how you really live. And that's when backstock enters the chat.

Backstock is more than some buzzword we throw around—it's a crucial part of maintenance and can save you time, money, and sanity. To further illustrate our point, we asked a few clients to weigh in on the topic. Here's what they had to say:

- "Backstock means no longer making unnecessary trips to the store, which are such a waste of time and send me into a panic. Now when I run out of something, I just swing by the backstock bin and get on with my day. No long checkout lines to wait in. No awkward parking situations to navigate. I have enough problems."

- "I save more money buying in bulk because I have more time to research prices and find the best deals out there."
- "I'm the designated shopper in my family, and backstock helps me keep track of what items are being used, and what I should never buy again. There's no way I can rely on my family for that information. Are you kidding me?"
- "Backstock allows me to stay ready, so I don't have to get ready. Example: My kid always forgets about a school project until the night before it is due, and since most projects require a poster board, I save future me the trouble and stock up this year."

Time, money, sanity, and systems that stick—who knew that backstock had so many benefits? Oh, right, we did . . . and now so do you!

HARDWIRING YOUR HABITS

Scrolling through TikTok in bed every morning. Eating chocolate after dinner. Putting things back where they belong. Habits become hardwired in our brain whether they are helpful or harmful. If you do something enough times, you forget you are even doing it—which can be the greatest gift or the biggest curse, depending on your mindset.

But let's take a step back, shall we? Why is it that our so-called bad habits are easier to form than good ones? It's because human beings are motivated by instant reward, and you better believe we're choosing the path of least resistance to get there! Understanding this puts us back in the driver's seat and gives us more control—another thing our brains love—with updated strategies for our long-term success.

Building one small habit at a time makes it more likely to stick, but especially when you layer that new habit on top of an already-established habit. For example:

- Putting your makeup away while brushing your teeth
- Hanging up your bag as you walk in the door and take off your shoes (assuming taking off your shoes is an already-established habit; if not, turn to page 46 for more on that)
- Emptying the dishwasher while the coffee is brewing
- Folding your clean laundry while watching your favorite show
- Checking expiration dates while eating a snack
- Deleting emails while waiting in the carpool line

Like working out or eating healthy, organizing is the gift that keeps on giving; if you form the habit, you can remind yourself of the benefit, even when you are dreading the task.

ENTRY

DIFFICULTY LEVEL: ★☆☆☆☆☆☆☆☆☆

Y*ou never get a second chance to make a good first impression.* We've all heard that phrase a million times, and we couldn't disagree more. I mean, why would a person even get out of bed in the morning if they didn't believe in second chances? But when it comes to your entry, that old cliché about first impressions is true. Which can feel like a lot of pressure to get it right.

No matter where or how you live, you have an entry. Maybe you live in a huge house, and your entry is a grand foyer with a double closet, fancy marble floors, and a pretty round table with a humongous, seasonally appropriate floral arrangement in the center (just dreaming here). Or maybe you live in a studio apartment and your entry is a teeny-tiny shelf with a hook for your keys that's mounted to your living room wall. Most entryways, however, fall in between those two extremes. No matter the size, though, your entry is your hello and your goodbye. It's the space that sends you off in the morning feeling like you have your act together, and the little cozy embrace that greets you when you come home at the end of the day. And yes, it has its own moods. Meaning, depending on the day, your entry can swing widely from "I'm Absolutely Unstoppable" to "I'm Pretty Sure I'm Wearing Two Different Black Shoes."

Why is it so hard to keep the entry organized? Um . . . life? If your house is filled with other people, there are umbrellas that don't close, mail that no one has opened, soccer cleats or softball gloves or lacrosse sticks that are forever in the way (please *please* can someone invent a foldable lacrosse stick?). If you live alone, there are purses that would rather go on the kitchen counter than on the hook by the door and car keys that want to take a field trip to your bedroom from time to time.

But we're here to tell you that you *can* get a second chance to make a good first impression. At least where your entry is concerned. It just requires the right maintenance—and by *right*, we mean the one that fits your space and your lifestyle. So, come on in, leave your shoes by the door, and let's get started.

FIVE MESSY ENTRY EXCUSES, DEBUNKED

1 *"Mornings are so hectic in my house that it takes too long to go hunting for things in bins."*

Before you forget about bins altogether, ask yourself, Is it the overall solution that isn't working for us or just how we're using them? It might be that your categories are too broad or too specific, or half of what you're sifting through doesn't belong there in the first place. But here's the real kicker: Are the bins labeled? Because if not, then of course you are having to hunt to find things! Labels are basically huge road signs that read, "HEY!! HERE I AM!!!!" and no one has to relearn how to use a map (thanks, GPS!).

2 *"My door opens right into my living room so I literally have no place to put mail and packages or anything that's bigger than my keys!"*

Take advantage of vertical space with a wall unit! From hooks to cubbies, you can easily find an option that fits your needs and also matches the aesthetic of your home.

3 *"The second they come home, my kids dump their stuff right beside the front door and are on to the next thing. It makes me crazy, but I can't be monitoring them every time they step into the house."*

Try tweaking the system to meet your kids where they are. Forget the hooks, forget the cubbies. Grab some open bins and place them right by the front door. That way, whatever the kids drop will have a contained place to land.

4 *"I have a hall closet, but I also have a blended family of seven, and everybody has activities that require stuff. There's just no way to corral it all in the closet, and we need all of it."*

First things first . . . we know you need all of the items, but do they all need to live in the hall closet? As a general rule, this space should be reserved for items you access daily (or multiple times a week!). If it ends up you are accessing all these items frequently, create more space by adding an over-the-door unit and stackable storage solutions.

5 *"When I get home at the end of the day, I'm too tired to put things back where they are supposed to go. I'm not lazy! I'm just not motivated enough."*

We get it. This just means that your system is too complicated or doesn't flow properly with your routine. Be honest with yourself. What can you realistically maintain? Meet yourself where you are and feel no guilt about it.

THE FUNDAMENTALS CHECKLIST FOR ANY ENTRY

Need to have:

- A place for frequently worn shoes
- A flat surface to sort mail
- A grab-and-go space for keys, sunglasses, wallet or purse
- Hanging space for in-season coats

Nice to have:

- A chair or bench (for putting on shoes)
- Hanging system for backpacks and tote bags
- Storage for pet needs
- Activity storage (for everything from water bottles to soccer cleats)
- Receptacle for incoming/outgoing packages
- Extra hanging and storage space for guests
- Someone on hand to immediately take your things and put them away (*kidding* . . . kind of?)

WATCH THE TRAFFIC

No matter how people enter your home (front door, back door, kitchen door, garage door—anything we're missing here?!), remember that it's a *high-traffic space*. As people come in and go out, so do their shoes, jackets, backpacks, purses, keys, wallets, sunglasses, umbrellas—the list goes on and on, changes with the seasons, and differs for every household.

Since the entry is the first thing people see when they walk into your home, it's tempting to focus strictly on aesthetics. But the truth is that no matter what type of entry you have, if you don't think through your flow of traffic, *like really, really think through it from every angle*, your system will be full of roadblocks, speed bumps, and other annoying distractions you don't have time for.

DESIGNATED DROP SPOT

Here's a great example of a standard mudroom. This one makes us smile not only because it's beautiful (we *always* appreciate a matching basket/wood paneling moment) but also because in one compact space, it hits on many objectives that make an entry work: use of vertical space for lesser-used items, dedicated hooks and baskets for each family member, and labels, labels, labels—aka easy-to-read instructions for everyone in the household.

It also has concealed drawer storage down below, which means that the youngest family member, the one who isn't tall enough to reach the hooks yet, has little excuse as to why they can't use and somehow benefit from this system. *(Meet them at their level, literally!)*

But wait . . . here's what you need to remember about concealed storage when it comes to maintenance. It's a dream that can quickly turn into a dumping ground nightmare if you're not careful. We're talking junk drawers, but full of things that never even made it to the kitchen. So, if you're the type of person who lives by the mantra "If I can't see the mess, it's not there," then concealed drawers might not be for you. May we suggest clear bins, instead?

SHEP
SUNDAY
FORD
purses
misc

THE TWO-FOR-ONE

If you're supertight on space, or your front door opens right into your living room (hello, studio apartments everywhere), thoughtfully tricking out the piece of furniture that serves as your entry will transport you to that magical sweet spot where form *and* function meet. The secrets to making a freestanding unit work are as follows:

- edit edit edit
- avoid piling things on top of and around the piece
- focus on the *everyday* (your can't-leave-home-without-them items)
- follow the 80/20 rule: keep your home no more than 80 percent full and leave space for things that might be entering your home, even if they're not there yet. Unless, of course, you are one of the two or three people on the planet who don't shop online. *(Which, if so, what do you do? Just . . . walk into a store?!)*

TIP

If you are looking to elevate your entryway, just add wallpaper. Choose one that makes you feel calm and happy whenever you see it so you can put your best foot forward every time you walk in and out the front door.

THE MUDROOMLESS MUDROOM...

Also known as the hall closet. This is the space in many homes where too-small coats and mateless mittens go to die a sad, lonely death. And you know—*we* know—that you can do better. Remember: When you're having trouble maintaining a space, it probably means that you're not allowing flexibility into your system. We've said it before, but it bears repeating (honestly, we could repeat this on every single page of this book): Organizing is not a one-and-done proposition. It's like eating well, or working out, or maintaining relationships. It requires ongoing work, but we promise it's worth it!

Here we obviously have a family with little kids (I mean, those adorable rain boots!!), and everybody knows that one of the major problems with kids is that they refuse to stop growing. (For *much* more on that topic, see "Kids' Zones," page 92.) Which means you need to be hypervigilant in the high-use area known as the hall closet.

Constantly ask yourself: What really needs to be here? Do the towels get moved to the top shelf once summer is over? Do the water bottles need to go to the kitchen to make room for soccer cleats?

Color coding is helpful, as in any space, but the key is evolution: adding (e.g., more hooks or more baskets on the door as needed), subtracting (outgrown items throughout), revising (the all-important labels). With the right evolving maintenance, your system will never feel haphazard, but instead like a series of smart choices (or gold stars, if you will).

COLOR ORDER

Kids and adults can both follow a ROYGBIV (rainbow) order, which keeps this space bright and organized. For long-term maintenance, having options is key. In this case, an over-the-door system, labeled

baskets, tote bags, hangers, and divided shoe bins (which can also stack) present various solutions for different seasons and members of the household. Keeping kids' stuff where they can easily reach it is smart (and gives the adult in charge five extra minutes in the morning).

Extra credit: When is a tote bag not a tote bag? When it's "off duty" and hung in the closet to provide storage.

Remodelista
LIVING WITH WHITE
VICTORIA HAGAN LIVE NOW

TABLE IT

What's that, no mudroom, no closet, no hope? Nope, that attitude won't cut it here! If you have a table—a table! any kind of table!—that's all you need. Let's revisit our fundamentals, shall we? A place for frequently worn shoes: basket on the floor. A flat surface for sorting mail: umm . . . a *table*. A grab-and-go space for keys/wallet/sunglasses: Any attractive bowl or basket will do. And hanging space for in-season coats? Well, what you don't see is the vintage coatrack that's just out of frame (which yes, we were obsessed with and yes, haven't stopped talking about since).

Admittedly, this space looks pretty great. And believe it or not, the decorative items you see on the table-as-entry actually serve a very important function. Not only do they allow you to bring your unique style to a space, but as you maintain your system, they prevent you from loading up your table-entry with a lot of migrating, random items that don't belong there (looking at you, hairbrush). Beware of flat surfaces, that's all we're saying.

If your needs are greater than what we've listed above, feel free to add more floor baskets, or perhaps an acrylic file box with dividers for mail, magazines, even kids' homework in a pinch.

WHEN LIFE CHANGES BUT YOUR SYSTEMS DON'T

Here we have a creature commonly found in the domestic ecosystem, which is Mudroom Gone Wild. It's sort of like when you plant a garden (or so we hear?) and everything looks incredible . . . until the weeds start popping up. You need to pull those weeds if you want to give the flowers space to grow.

This homeowner has avoided the trap of overstuffing her baskets and cubbies as kids grow and activities mount, so kudos to her for that. (If bins are overflowing, that's your space holding you accountable.) There is still an airiness here, which can be hard in a busy house with a busy family. When we look at this mudroom, though, what we see is the remnants of a perfect system that couldn't keep up with the life of this family: shoes tossed more or less wherever, random items on shelves, footballs and soccer balls trying to make a break for it. Just add glitter or sand and you've got the stuff of nightmares.

Why this system WASN'T WORKING

- The kids couldn't quite reach the designated bins on the top shelf, which is why their items ended up everywhere *but there*.
- The initial idea was to keep the bench area clear, so the kids have a place to put on their shoes, but you know what we say about flat surfaces . . . dumping ground.
- The bottom cubbies were designated for shoes, but with such a large storage space to fill and no container in sight, yep, once again . . . dumping ground.
- The system hadn't evolved to accommodate new activities and items that come with it (i.e., athletic gear).

BEFORE

HOW WE UPDATED IT

- Since we couldn't shift the entire bin system down, we created a drop zone for kids on the bench. Sure, it means the adults have to transfer items at the end of the day, but far better than the alternative, don't you think?
- We added pillows/a throw blanket to the bench to give it a real purpose so it's not just an empty surface where things pile up.
- Wire bins in the lower cubbies now keep shoes and sports equipment contained within that space . . . even when thrown inside haphazardly.
- The repurposed vertical storage bay on the far left is the family's command center. Each kid has a designated file holder for homework, forms that need to be signed, etc., and we also included an inbox/outbox system for mail.
- The labeling system was in desperate need of an update, so we made some slight adjustments to match how the family is currently using the space.
- The bags on hooks are prepacked with items that the family members need for various activities: work, school, sports, games. Now getting out the door is as easy as grab-and-go.

AFTER

ALL TOGETHER NOW

Is it too much to assume that the happiness level in this household has doubled now that their mudroom is back on track? No, no it is not (which is why Joanna thinks of organizing as the best bang for your buck). You know the power of meeting people where they live, with a reasonable system at the ready, or you wouldn't be reading this book. When it comes to an entry, the idea is to learn where the people in your house naturally put their stuff, and then gently train them to do it in a way that's organized and smart.

Top Five Phrases to GET YOUR GUESTS TO TAKE OFF THEIR SHOES

1. "Do you like this fabulous basket I found at the store? Amazing, right? It fits shoes PERFECTLY. Try it!"
2. "You know what's so crazy? Those shoes have just been in public places and then just enter your house with *public places* germs on them. Anyway, feel free to leave yours by the door!"
3. "Our very naughty puppy (ahem, Indie Shearer) loves to eat shoes, so when you take them off, I'll make sure to put them in the closet."
4. "The phrase 'no shirt, no shoes, no service' is really overrated. I mean, keep your shirt on, but I'll happily take your shoes off your hands."
5. "Take your shoes off."

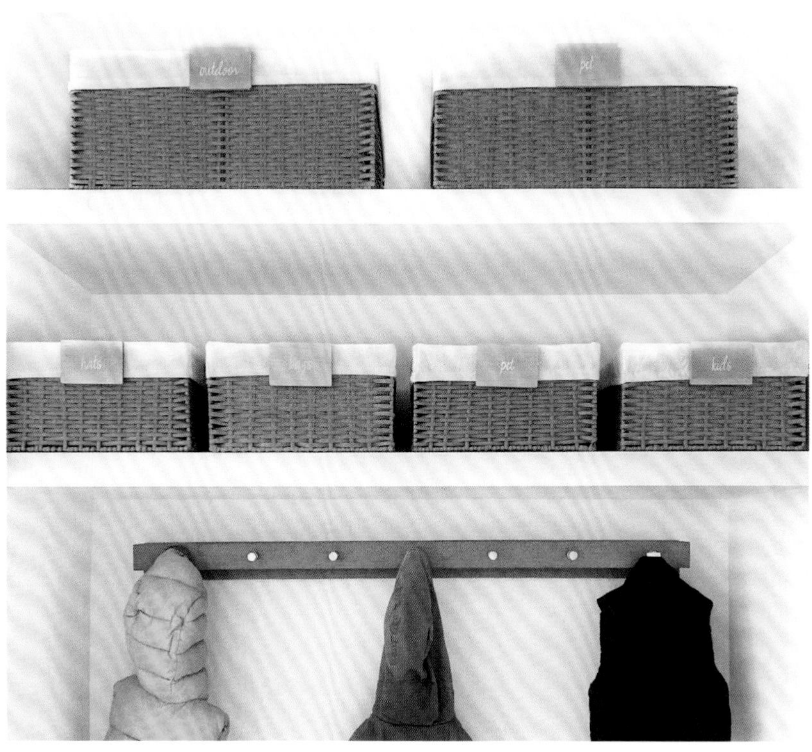

LOW-BAR LIFESTYLE LONG-TERM GOALS

- Understand that your entry is always going to be the most active space in your home. Make peace with the traffic flow and find ways to work with it.

- Give yourself permission to accept that you aren't going to nail organizing your entry as one and done. An organized entry is a *daily* process.

- Even if you live alone, know that your entry's needs will evolve as your life changes. Thoughtful anticipation is the name of the game.

LAUNDRY & UTILITY ROOM

DIFFICULTY LEVEL: ★★☆☆☆☆☆☆☆

Close your eyes for a second and imagine your life as a Venn diagram. Two circles: one labeled CLEAN and the other labeled ORGANIZED. In an ideal world (emphasis on *ideal*, people), your Venn diagram has a nearly 100 percent overlap—meaning your life is both clean and organized, all the time.

Your laundry room is where CLEAN and ORGANIZED come together. More than any other space in your house, this little room offers the promise of low-effort transformation. It's the you-get-a-do-over headquarters. Walk in dirty and come out clean (and folded!).

But in too many households, the laundry room becomes the dumping ground for all sorts of stuff that hasn't quite found its rightful home. It's like the garage, but inside your house. Especially if your laundry room is also a utility room, where you keep cleaning supplies, pet food, and lightbulbs. Depending on your individual laundry and cleaning needs, this room can end up being a throwaway space that you can ignore once the door is shut.

Or maybe you don't have a laundry room. If that's the case, we see you too, but you still need to organize your supplies.

Regardless of whether your laundry room is a big, bright space with room for sorting and folding, a small room with inadequate shelving, or just an over-the-door unit for your go-to supplies, laundry and cleaning need care, too. We may never convince you to love doing laundry (let's be honest, we only enjoy the folding part), but you can love the space where it happens.

LG
Steam
Direct Drive

FIVE MESSY LAUNDRY EXCUSES, DEBUNKED

1 *"I spend as little time as possible in the laundry room, so I honestly don't care what it looks like."*

But hear us out . . . what if you liked the way your laundry room looked? Just enjoyed the overall vibe? Sometimes, we don't even know something is stressing us out until it's replaced with something better.

2 *"My laundry room is where I keep cleaning supplies, and I've got such a mismatched collection of brooms and buckets and bottles that it's beyond help."*

We often find that when people love the way their space looks, they are more likely to maintain it. We give you our blessing to donate your old items and replace them with matching sets.

3 *"I don't have a laundry room! I keep all my cleaning supplies underneath my kitchen sink, which is the only place they'll fit!"*

Do you have a hall closet? Are you using the back of that door as a storage opportunity? If not, go grab an Elfa over-the-door unit . . . now. Who cares if you have a meeting in two minutes? Insert a bookmark, grab those keys, and head to the store! Treat yourself to lunch after! Don't let the word *install* scare you . . . it takes three minutes, and even we can do it.

4 *"My laundry room is part laundry, part household cleaning, part pet care, and part weekend project station. It has too many functions that I can't keep track of, and they all seem to overlap."*

You, friend, are in desperate need of zones. Broad zones. General zones. Zones that are so user-friendly that even the person who puts pretzels in the "nuts" canister can figure them out. From there, you can subcategorize how you use and search for the items.

5 *"I have a huge hamper in the laundry room, but my kids just throw everything on the floor. Even clean clothes they take out of the dryer!"*

There needs to be a quick pipeline from where your kids tend to throw their clothes and where the hampers are located. Each kid needs their own separate hamper depending on this. We know it would be easier for you if your family brought their laundry to where it will be washed, but we're meeting people where they live, right? It's worth taking those few extra steps.

THE FUNDAMENTALS CHECKLIST FOR ANY LAUNDRY/UTILITY ROOM

Need to have:

- Hamper or basket for dirty clothes
- Hamper or basket for clean clothes (or if you'd rather use the same basket as above, go for it!)
- Adequate storage for detergents, stain removal products, dryer sheets
- Adequate storage for cleaning supplies
- Trash can for dryer lint, clothing labels, etc.

Nice to have:

- Divided hamper system for various family members
- Table or counter for treating stains and folding clean clothes
- Zoned shelving for backstock

soap
soap
Tide
free & gentle
Tide
free & gentle
laundry
bath
sprays

CLEARLY BEAUTIFUL

No margin for error in the mess department here. The advantage of open shelving is that everything is clearly visible. The *disadvantage* of open shelving is that . . . everything is clearly visible.

You see where we're going with this. We love open shelving: easy-access, relatively mindless backstock inventory taking, opportunities to make things as weird and oddly shaped as cleaning products pretty when organized the right way. But if you're debating whether or not you're an open-shelving person, know that there are risks. We're not talking grave injury here (imagine an open shelf that comes with a liability form?), but you need to control your impulse to throw and go. You need to commit to keeping this up.

Enter the bin . . . which, if you haven't realized by now, is everyone's best friend. They're perfect for creating precisely labeled zones to corral items exactly how you use them (electric iron + detergent, for instance), they're easy to clean, and they're an ideal choice to cover an entire shelf surface—so you simply cannot cram extra stuff in the sides—while maintaining a visually neat space.

About these hampers: Fabric liners mean you can throw the liner in the wash with the clothes as needed, which is unbelievably helpful! But when it comes to anything spillable—detergent, sprays, liquid soaps—always go with storage that can be quickly wiped down when drip disasters strike.

TOP 5 WAYS TO ENCOURAGE USING THE HAMPER INSTEAD OF THE FLOOR

- Reward good behavior with gold stars and compliments.
- Move the hamper to the most convenient place in the room—even if it's right next to the door.
- Plead and beg.
- Complain loudly and often.
- Okay fine, resort to bribery.

DIY TO MVP

No shelves? No folding station? No laundry room? No problem. This all-in-one cart, perfect for anybody tight on space, can be tricked out to meet your needs, whatever they may be. Dual hampers keep darks and lights separate and can be rolled to the washing machine (or even your front door if you're headed to the Laundromat). The flat surface on top serves as easy-access storage for your basic (i.e., tightly edited) laundry needs and can double as a folding surface when the time comes. As your needs change, hooks can be added to the side for hanging clothes, assorted rags, desperation midchore snacks—you name it.

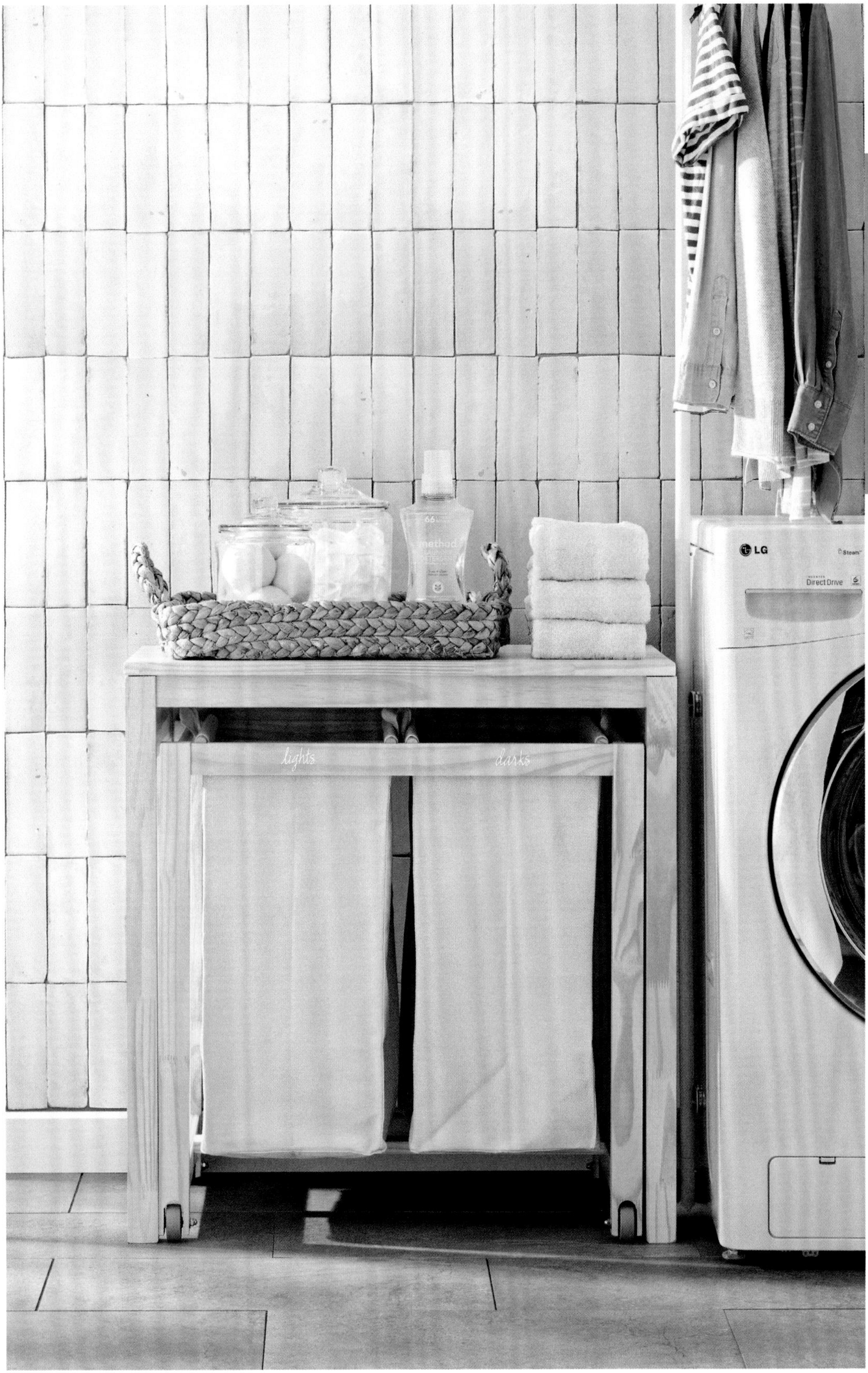
lights
darks
method
LG
Direct Drive

EXPLOSION IN THE UTILITY AISLE

Honestly, isn't that what this looks like? This photo is hard for us to talk about without some sort of breathing exercises and a Xanax.

Just kidding! Sadly, though, we know from experience that this is how lots of people deal with that random storage space when life gets busy and there's a door that closes. Where this family saw a closet under the stairs as a storage catchall, we saw catastrophe. But also, opportunity!

floor
floor
GLAD
GLAD
GLAD
bags
utility
lightbulbs
ever spring
ever spring
ever spring
wipes
Swiffer
Swiffer
DRY SWEEPING CLOTHS
DRY SWEEPING CLOTHS
floor
Grove Co.
Grove Co.
DAWN
soap
100%
method
method
method
floor
tissues
sprays
toilet paper
toilet paper

AFTER

DIVIDE AND CONQUER *(previous page)*

All we needed to turn that understair horror show into this dream space was some shelving, baskets and bins, clear labels, and a plan. This Elfa system is affordable and adjustable, and it can change with needs and seasons—meaning no strict, lifetime rules about spacing for the commitment-phobic. A clever Elfa utility track on the wall keeps items off the floor and out of the way and can be easily customized to grab just about anything. Clear plastic bins are perfect for things that look good—who knew Mr. Clean could be so visually pleasing? (Is he a genie? A sailor? Does anyone even know?) And for things that are less attractive, woven baskets can store vacuum attachments and toilet paper (toss the rolls in the basket, and they make bathroom restocking a cinch—just take the basket with you).

APARTMENT THERAPY

This is a sanity saver for anyone whose "utility closet" is that weird little sliver of space next to the refrigerator where dust bunnies go to reproduce. Even if you don't have the luxury of space for a cleaning caddy, the right mounted system can hold bottles, rags, brooms, and more. You don't *have* to ROYGBIV your products (but you've got to admit it looks even better when you do).

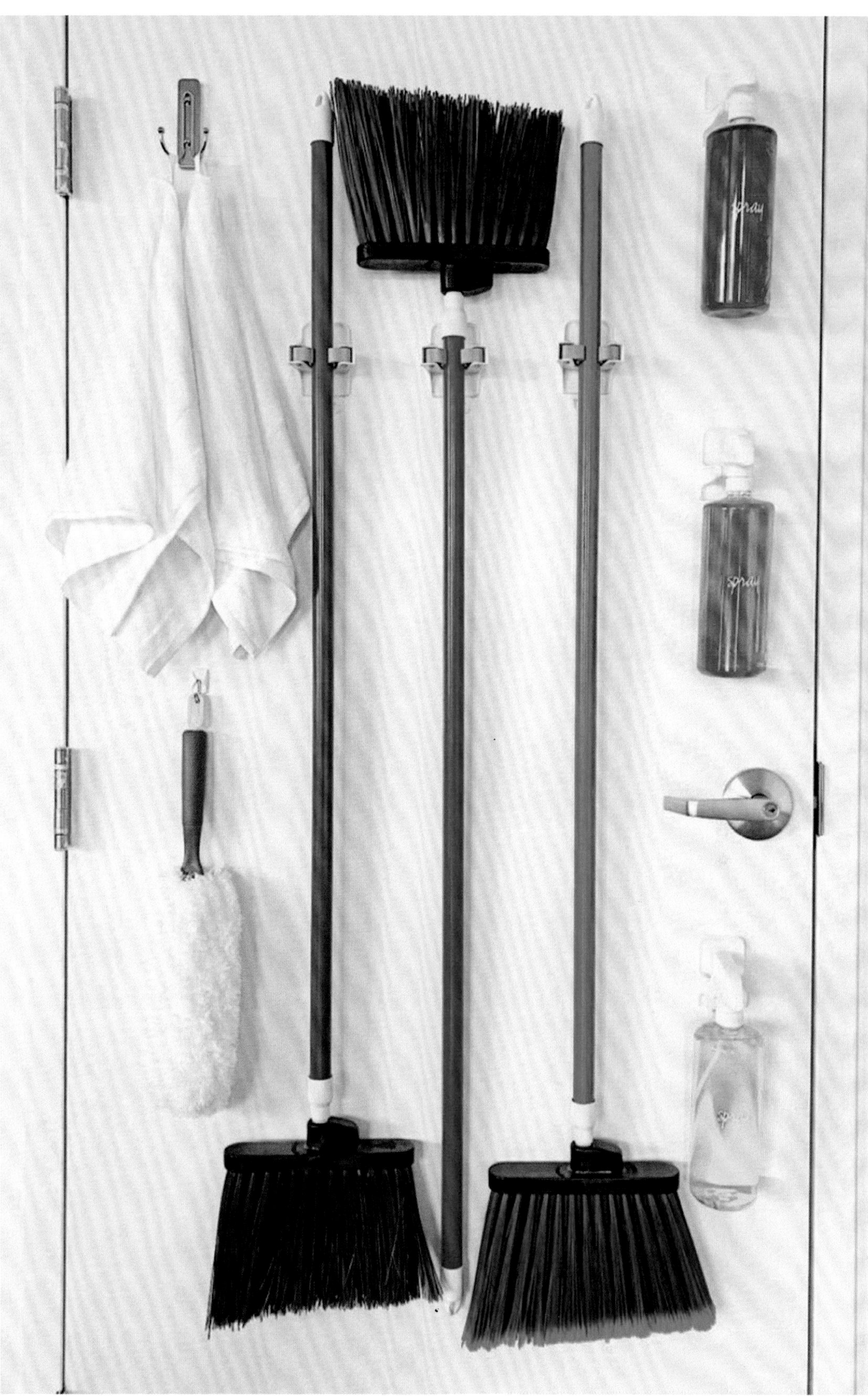
spray
spray

Clips

etc.
WASH & STAIN
BAR

LOW-BAR LIFESTYLE LONG-TERM GOALS

Just because they're dry doesn't mean they need to be folded immediately—let your clothes live in the dryer until you're ready to tackle them. They take up *way* more physical space in a big messy pile on your bed.

- If your house has more than one floor, keep a little cleaning caddy on each level for low-stress motivation and ease of use.

- If you have the space, keep a "deal with it on the weekend" receptacle for random dirty items (e.g., those rags you use to wipe your dog's paws) that don't need immediate attention. Unwashed laundry sitting in the machine and staring at you = PRESSURE.

- Always remember that your low-bar practices can lead to high-bar moments. Invest in smart, organized laundry room backstock, and you never need to spend time on a frustrating search for that lightbulb/battery/stain stick the moment you need it. Organized people are just too lazy to look for things.

FLAT SURFACES TO USE AS A FOLDING STATION IN A PINCH

(Good for: newborn clothes, underwear, socks. Not advisable for: beach towels, tablecloths, XXL men's pants.)

- Laptop
- Cutting board
- FedEx box
- Top of filing cabinet
- Three-ring binder
- Cookie sheet
- This book

BATHROOM

DIFFICULTY LEVEL: ★★★☆☆☆☆☆☆

Here's where we make a joke about needing a bathroom break. Barely four chapters into our journey!! You really can't take us anywhere, can you??!?

The truth is that everyone uses a bathroom multiple times a day, in many different ways. Which makes it a high-traffic space in the home, where people are generally rushing to get out the door, or into bed. Which *also* makes it easier for your family to ignore all your organizing efforts, whether they intend to or not.

And you might be part of the problem, too! Sorry, but as Lizzo says, truth hurts! After all, your life is busy and your bathroom reflects that, with its bottles and cans and towels and tubes, all with various uses and expiration dates. Even if your mornings involve no more than moisturizer, deodorant, and a toothbrush—you still need toothpaste. And probably floss. See what a slippery slope a bathroom can be? And if you wear makeup, you're *definitely* part of the problem (speaking from experience here). Yep, we see you. Unfortunately, we also see all those samples and possibly expired products that you are holding on to for the just-in-case day when you will use them. News flash: "just-in-case day" is probably never coming. And eighty little sample bottles make our 80/20 rule *much* harder to follow.

FIVE MESSY BATHROOM EXCUSES, DEBUNKED

BATHROOM

1 *"I share a bathroom with my husband, who leaves everything on the countertop instead of back in the drawer . . . WHERE EVERYTHING HAS A HOME!!!"*

It's safe to say your husband is a "counter person." Are you willing to be the one who puts things back in the drawer where they "belong" every day for the rest of your life? If yes, then keep your system as is. If not? Place a divided turntable on the countertop, and he can store all his essentials there. Sure, it's still an eyesore, but at least it's contained.

2 *"My four kids share a bathroom, but don't share products since they are all different ages and at different stages . . . HELP!!"*

You'll probably hate us for this . . . but you must start by removing everything from the space and staging a proper edit. Group the items belonging to each kid, categorize them, and most likely, find a ton of almost-empty bottles. Toss those, designate physical zones of storage, use stackable or vertical options to save space, and go pour yourself a glass of champagne.

3 *"My bathroom is so small—I can't even figure out where to store my hair dryer, much less toilet paper backstock. Too many of the things I use every day just have to live on the edge of the sink."*

Living life on the edge, literally. Don't worry, the solution is simple. As long as you have a door on your bathroom, you have storage to use. Also, never underestimate the power of a rolling cart in a small space. Just saying.

4 *"My linen closet has to accommodate everything from sunscreen bottles to king-size sheets, and it's bursting at the seams."*

Some of those sheets might be bursting at the seams, too. When was the last time you edited?

5 *"I never met a beauty product I didn't like, and my bathroom drawers are full of stuff I still haven't used. But it feels wasteful to throw away good products."*

Same, but keep reading . . . you'll have a whole new perspective after reading this chapter. Because we did.

THE FUNDAMENTALS CHECKLIST FOR ANY BATHROOM

Need to have:

- Organized, easy access for daily-use items like brushes, toothpaste, razors
- Caddy or shelving to corral items in the shower
- Designated zones for categories/family members
- User-friendly system to hold frequently used cosmetics
- Backstock space for extra toilet paper rolls

Nice to have:

- Under-the-sink storage for lesser used products
- Closet or shelving for extra towels
- Turntables for beauty products
- Go-to bin or drawer for guests
- A promise from your messy family members that they will find someplace else to shower and brush their teeth so you can actually have this bathroom to yourself, forever

BIN THERE, DONE THAT

If folding isn't your thing, bins are your answer. Towels rolled and neatly contained look just as good as a perfectly folded stack, especially when choosing storage that matches your aesthetic. But it's not just a design choice! When your products match, you can trick yourself into thinking that this is décor, not everyday items, and be more likely to maintain them. (Yes, playing mind games with yourself is encouraged if it leads to better-looking shelves.) As far as actual décor pieces, like the clock and mirror seen here? Again, not just a design choice, but a way to prevent the dreaded "empty flat surface syndrome," in which random items that don't belong in the space migrate there and take up permanent residence.

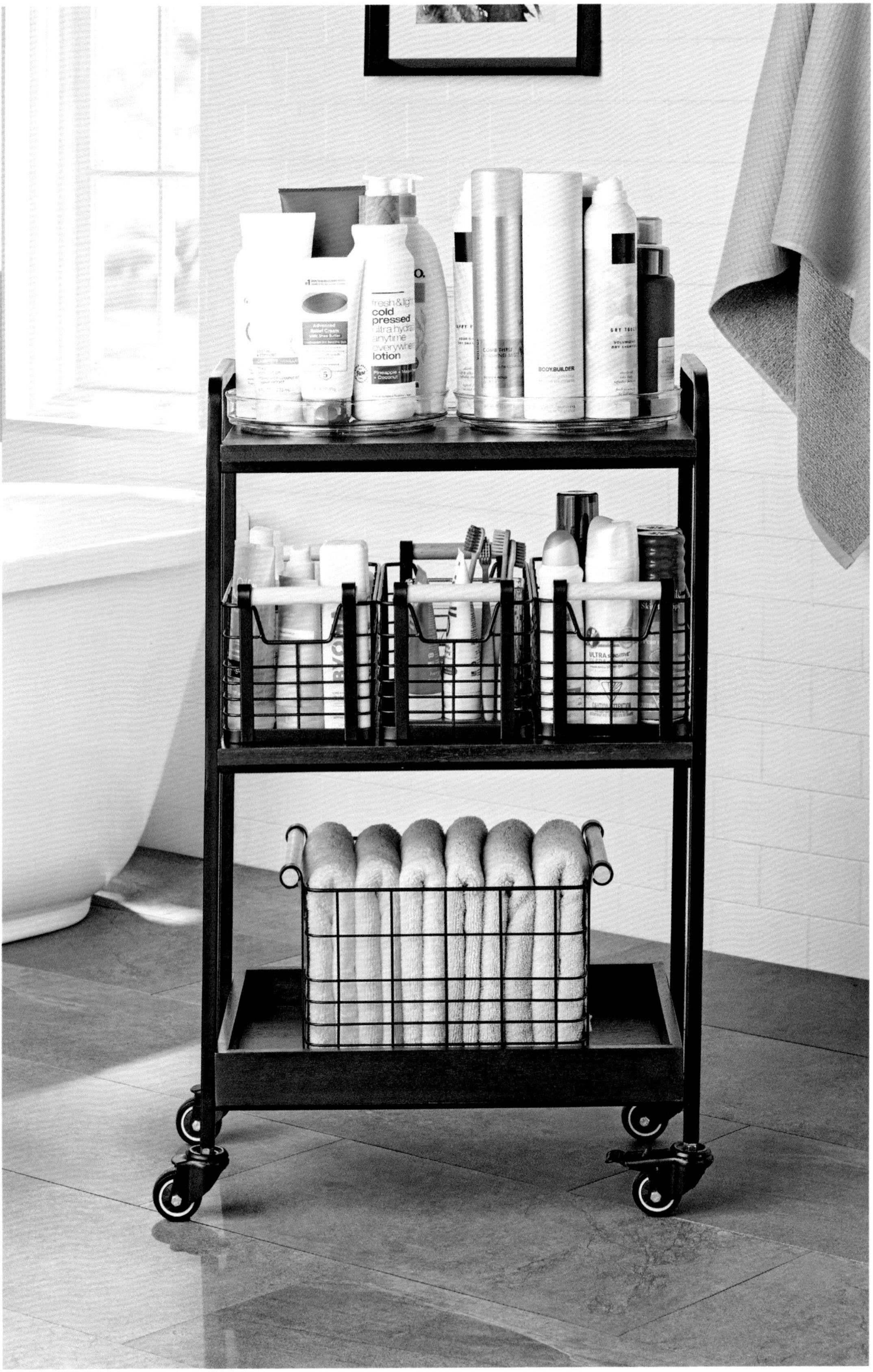
cold
pressed
lotion
BODY.BUILDER

THE SMART CART

When your bathroom has zero storage space, it can add a whole other layer of frustration to your day. You never really feel like you can "clean up"—which isn't ideal for people like us who thrive on checking things off their list. We see you creating designated zones for the items perched on your sink, but how about we flush that plan down the drain and try a cart instead? Yes, what's better and more convenient than a cabinet on wheels!?! Just make sure to categorize and contain within bins, or else it's no longer a cart, it's a hot mess express.

IF YOU MUST SHARE

Whether you're sharing with a partner or maintaining a shared kids' bathroom, everybody needs to have clearly labeled space of their own and be held accountable for keeping it up. If you're setting up a system for a spouse or a child, be realistic about their products and how often they use them. And be realistic about your expectations: Make sure the system *you* set up is easy for *them* to maintain. And try to resist the urge to constantly monitor what goes on in their drawers and bins. As long as they respect the boundaries of their space, you should be able to live with it. Which is why we taught our husbands early on that breaching the imaginary line that divides our bathroom space would be considered an act of war.

hair
face
makeup
hair
Batiste
DRY SHAMPOO
TROPICAL
FEKKAI
NOT YOUR MOTHER'S
Clean Freak
REFRESHING DRY SHAMPOO
KEVIN.MURPHY
BEDROOM.HAIR
PACIFICA
VEGAN CERAMIDE
WAKE UP BEAUTIFUL
VEGAN CREAM
MAYBELLINE
LASH SENSATIONAL
KEVIN.MURPHY
ANTI.GRAVITY
HAIRITAGE
PROTEIN TREATMENT

Goodfellow &CO
SPF 30 Face Lotion
HARRY'S
Exfoliating Face Wash
Leaves skin feeling clean and refreshed
5.1 fl oz / 150 ml
HARRY'S
Shave Cream
Cushions your shave & conditions your skin
with aloe & eucalyptus
3.4 fl oz / 100 ml
travel
travel
body
DUKE CANNON
TRENCH WARFARE
PRESCOTT
SENECA
toilet paper

YES, BEAUTY IS FLEETING

Believe it or not, a lot of people treat their beauty products like clothes. They hold on to things they never wear just because they feel bad getting rid of them. The difference is that while clothing goes out of style, beauty products (and some toiletries) actually expire. Not only do they lose effectiveness over time but they also become a breeding ground for bacteria. Skin infections? Pink eye? No thanks, we'll pass! Some containers will have icons that indicate when a product is past its prime ("6M" = six months), but some won't. Keep this helpful shelf-life guide on hand so you know when to toss a product and treat yourself to something new.

Toss after one month:
makeup sponges

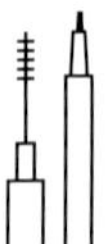

Toss after three months:
liquid eyeliner, mascara

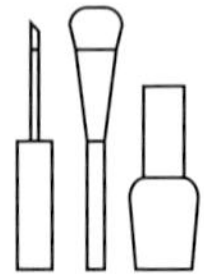

Toss after a year:
concealer, cream blush, eye shadow, foundation, lip gloss, nail polish

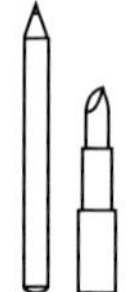

Toss after two years:
eyeliner pencil, lip balm, lipstick, powder blush

Tip: Write the date you open a product on the packaging to avoid any guesswork. And if you start noticing a change in texture, color, or smell before the expiration date? Toss it.

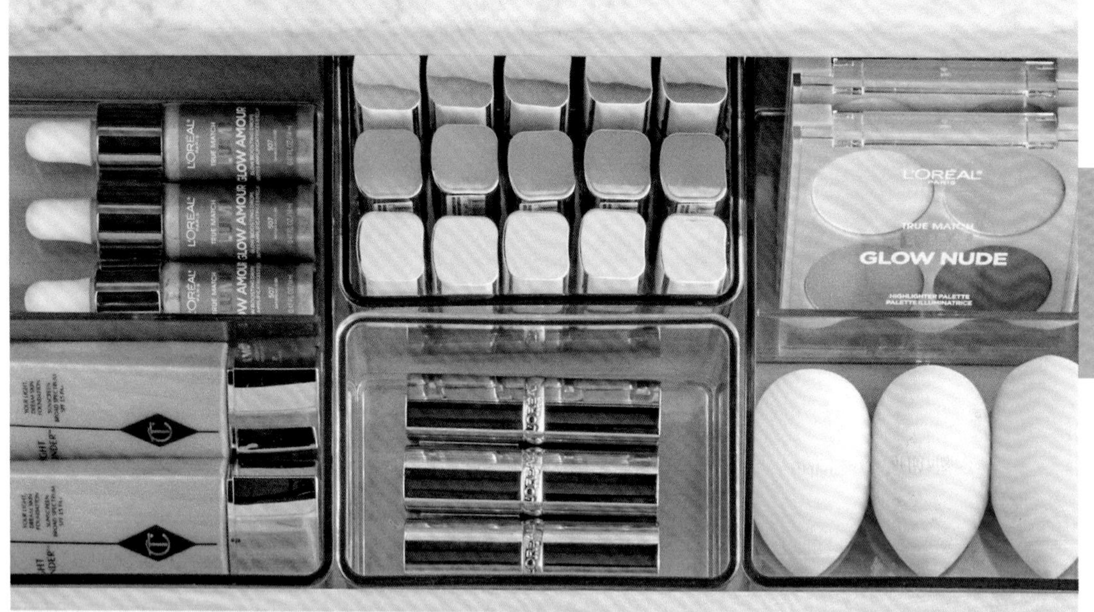
L'ORÉAL
TRUE MATCH
GLOW AMOUR
L'ORÉAL
TRUE MATCH
GLOW NUDE
HIGHLIGHTER PALETTE
PALETTE ILLUMINATRICE

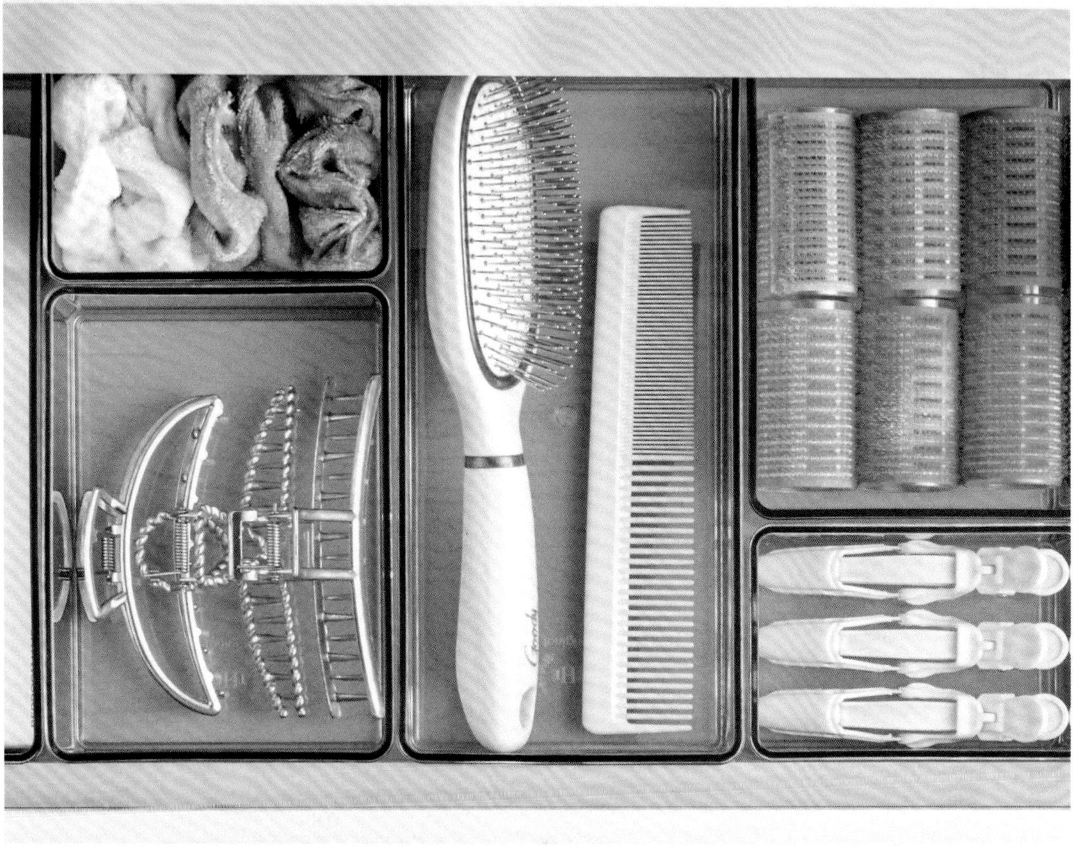

DO YOU REALLY NEED THAT

______________________*(fill in blank new product)*?

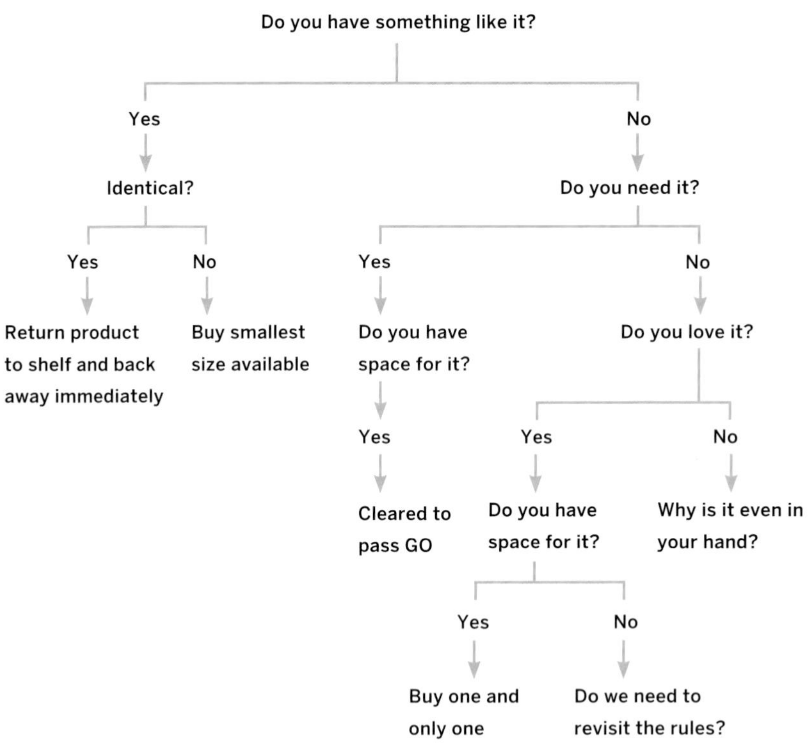

CLEAN SWEEP

If you don't have the luxury of a shower shelf or bench, a hanging shower caddy works just as well if not better. First, it keeps you honest: no hoarding products, or else bottles end up on the floor. Second, a divided caddy is perfect for sharing—everybody gets a shelf allotment. And if you're a person who likes to switch out products from time to time (variety is the spice of life— we love products, too!!), do not attempt to keep them all in the shower. This is one time when backstock is *not* your friend. Instead, set up a designated bin for them in your cabinet and switch them out when necessary.

BE KIND TO YOUR SHELF

Sometimes, a door you can close is the kindness you need in your week. It gives you temporary relief when you don't have the time to deal with something quite yet.

This client made good use of her space, but she had allowed random items to invade the shelves (looking at you . . . power drill?!). She also had fallen prey to a common problem, which was a reluctance to get rid of towels and sheets that were well past their prime (one was bleached and the other ripped—need we say more?).

BEFORE

Remember, people . . . the local animal shelter almost certainly can use your old towels. And if the prospect of that goodwill still doesn't move you, at least put your old linens to work in your utility room.

Because our client didn't have time to fold everything perfectly—which is becoming the theme of this chapter—we needed a solution where towels and sheets were easy to access but concealed. Now baskets with bin clips act as drawers for quick grab and go. (If you too are folding challenged, see How to Fold a Fitted Sheet on page 90.) And a hamper that's no longer see-through acts like a closed door for laundry.

NOT YOUR MOTHER'S

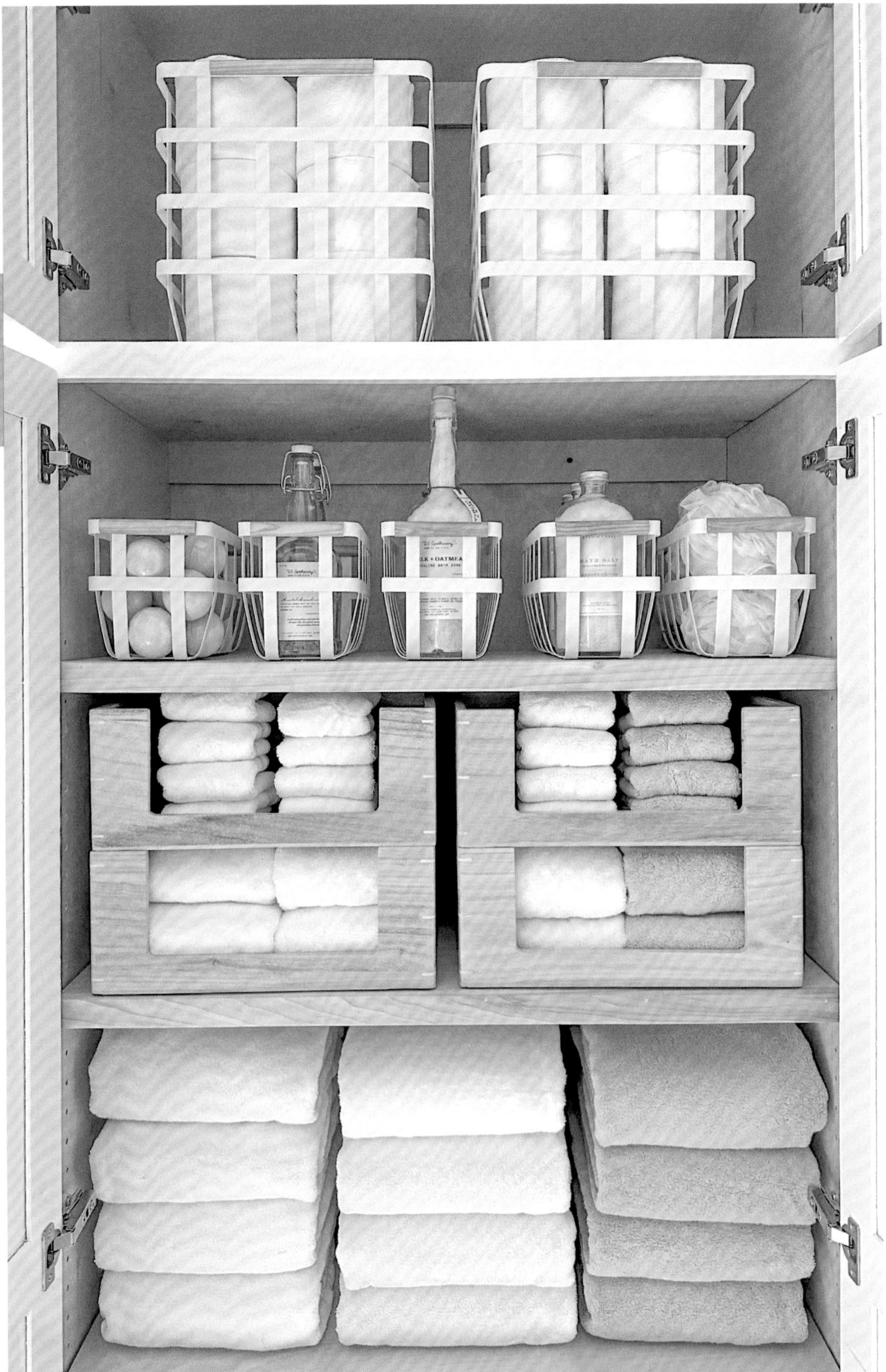

LOST IN SPACE

If you have deep cabinets like these, you may know the danger of a seemingly limitless space that beckons you with the promise of tremendous storage and peace of mind. Don't fall for it! Turns out that promise is false. If you need proof, know that we pulled 67 (!) towels out of this deep cabinet, and you don't need us to tell you that there is no family on earth who needs 67 towels. Oh, and the toilet paper was *behind* the towels. When is backstock not backstock? When it's stuck behind 67 towels.

Sometimes you just have to accept the fact that you aren't going to use all of your space—in other words, empty space is not a storage opportunity. For deep cabinets, know that easily accessed bins placed within reach are going to make maintenance much easier than trying to use the vast expanse behind them.

KNOW YOUR CUSTOMER

What's the key to successful kids' bathroom maintenance? Never enter the room without your choice of caffeine coursing through your veins. Or at the very end of the day when you're exhausted and cranky. Or any time in between.

Now, while this approach may work for some families, it's not altogether realistic. Which is why the key for successful kids' bathroom maintenance is as follows:

- Think about your customer. How does your kid work? The answer to this will vary by age and temperament, not to mention available space.

- Hold the users accountable. If even a three-year-old can put a toothbrush back in a cup, just think what a thirteen-year-old is capable of.

- Finally, learn when to care and not to care. Make it clear to your child that you have certain standards, but don't be so strict that you're setting them up for failure. They need to follow house rules—and you need to be flexible.

GUEST SERVICES

Whether you like it or not, the powder room is one of the most important rooms in your house; it's often the only bathroom guests will see. No pressure! Luckily, people don't spend a lot of time here. Your only goal, other than to make sure the space is clean and stocked with soap and hand towels, is to keep necessities within reach. When a guest in your home is forced to ask where the toilet paper is, it's awkward for everyone involved.

GUEST LECTURE

You probably know by now that "start with a drawer" is one of our organizing pillars. When it comes to maintenance, sometimes the thought of tackling an entire room (or even a closet within a room) is so overwhelming, it stops you in your tracks. That's why we love the guest bathroom. Look at this beautiful drawer! Even if you have visitors only once a year, even if your guest bathroom cabinet is nothing more than a pretty organized bin filled with essentials, you can still set up a clearly labeled system to make someone feel welcome and taken care of. And you can make yourself feel accomplished and ready to tackle a larger space with confidence.

towels
towels
toilet paper

BATHROOM

HOW TO FOLD A FITTED SHEET: 10 EASY STEPS!

Step 1: Grab your fitted sheet with the elastic facing out.

Step 2: Fight back tears while wishing you had longer arms or just more hands.

Step 3: Find the two corners on the long edge and flip them inside out.

Step 4: Put your hands inside the corners. Fold your right hand over your left.

Step 5: No, your other left. But we've already made it this far, *just keep swimming*.

Step 6: Swap hands, slide your other hand down, and match the corners.

Step 7: Contemplate starting over because the corners aren't matching up perfectly but ultimately decide to *just keep swimming.*

Step 8: Realize you have to repeat the same step on the other side and send out an SOS to your family and the entire neighborhood.

Step 9: Crickets. Guess it's just you and this sheet against the world now.

Step 10: Set your sheet down on a flat surface, realize you'll never make this octagon look like a neat square, cut your losses, and hide it in a decorative bin on a shelf instead.

LOW-BAR LIFESTYLE LONG-TERM GOALS

- Folding isn't your thing? Store in bins instead!

- Again, for the folding-averse: Hooks for towels are a great solution for kids or adults. That leaves the perfectly arranged towel on the bar for display only!

- If you have a product that you never use but can't bear to throw out because you spent good money on it, *drop the guilt*. Remind yourself that you're just doubling down on a mistake if you bought the wrong thing and are now letting it take up valuable space in your life.

- Place a tray on your countertop that acts as a temporary containment zone for items when you are running late and don't have time to put things back neatly in their actual home.

- Always keep at least three rolls of toilet paper on hand. No explanation needed.

KIDS' ZONES

DIFFICULTY LEVEL: ★★★★☆☆☆☆☆

Cognitive dissonance. It's what happens when you try to hold two opposing ideas in your brain at once. And it's what happens to us every time we walk into our kids' rooms. We love our kids truly, madly, and deeply while simultaneously feeling truly, madly, deeply annoyed by all their stuff. The clothes all over the floor, the toys strewn about willy-nilly, and don't even get us started on all the electronic devices. . . . But don't worry, we are here to help. And you don't even have to evict your kids in the process.

We get that you just . . . Can't. Deal. With. The. Stuff. We understand! I mean, by this point our kids are pretty well ~~brainwashed~~ trained, but that took years of ~~badgering threatening~~ gentle guidance on our parts.

Trust us when we tell you that if we can do it, you can do it! We're not saying you have to give in to the mess . . . but you do have to be realistic. There are very few circumstances when we would give this kind of advice for dealing with other people, but when dealing with kids, the trick is that you have to stoop to their level. Not literally, but figuratively. Try to understand how they see and use the items that make up their world. Communicating with a toddler is quite different from communicating with a teenager (well, mostly; sometimes the tantrums look oddly similar), and your approach to helping them maintain their stuff should be tailored accordingly.

Finally, bear in mind that a kids' space—perhaps more than any other space in your house—is where you need to find the middle ground. Where you can feel like your home is organized while allowing your child to have some measure of control and ownership, too. Although it's perfectly reasonable to insist that the middle ground is free of clothes.

FIVE MESSY KIDS' ZONE EXCUSES, DEBUNKED

1 *"I can talk to my kids until I'm blue in the face about keeping their rooms neat, and it's like I'm speaking in a foreign language. I'm tired of nagging them all the time."*

We're not saying to trick your kids, but we *are* saying to create systems that they won't even realize they are using. Which is different.

2 *"We live in a small house and our kids share a bedroom. The only way I could keep their room neat would be to get rid of all of their things."*

Unfortunately (and trust us, we *mean* unfortunately), kids come with things. Their dolls come with things. Their kits come with things. Things, things, things, all the things. The best plan of action is to stay on top of the action by taking away any mess-making opportunities. Pare down items and designate containment zones for them, whether it's throwing stuffed animals in a floor bin or adding functional wall shelving. If you don't make it clear to your kids where items should be put away, their first guess will always be the floor.

3 *"I have three school-age kids who seem to outgrow their clothes and shoes at a record-setting rate. Our household is too busy to stay organized."*

We can assure you that it's not! You just need to tweak the system to account for all these moving parts. For instance, setting up designated zones for items on their way in and on their way out.

4 *"My kids receive so many toys from their grandparents, and I don't know how to tell them to stop. They especially love gifting things that are big, bulky, and battery operated."*

Feel free to pass them this list.

GIFTS YOU SHOULD NEVER GIVE A CHILD, UNLESS YOU'RE TRYING TO PUNISH THE PARENTS

- Anything that makes noise
- Anything with more than 400 pieces
- Anything that requires more than an Allen wrench to assemble
- Anything containing or pertaining to slime or glitter

5 *"I have two teenage daughters and their bedrooms are a complete disaster. They have clothes and beauty products and schoolwork strewn all over the place. There is no way they are ever going to keep their rooms neat, so why even bother trying."*

We're meeting them where they live, right? Start by changing how you talk about it. Focus on what visual benefits a solution brings. Or say you saw it on TikTok. Think more "This stackable shoe storage can display all your favorite shoes!" and less "Put your shoes here or else . . ."

balls
balls

blocks
blocks

toys
toys

balls
balls

blocks
blocks

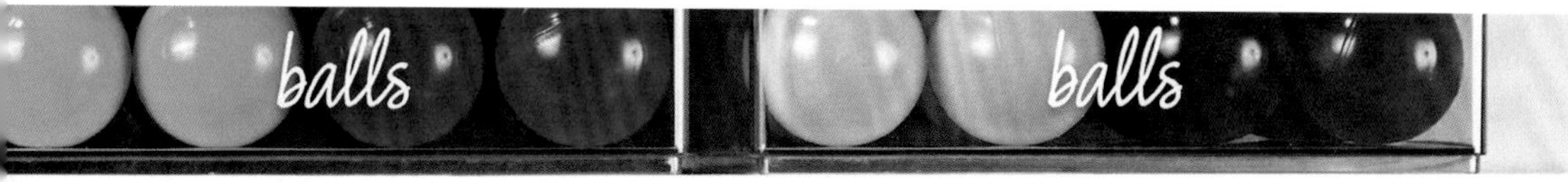

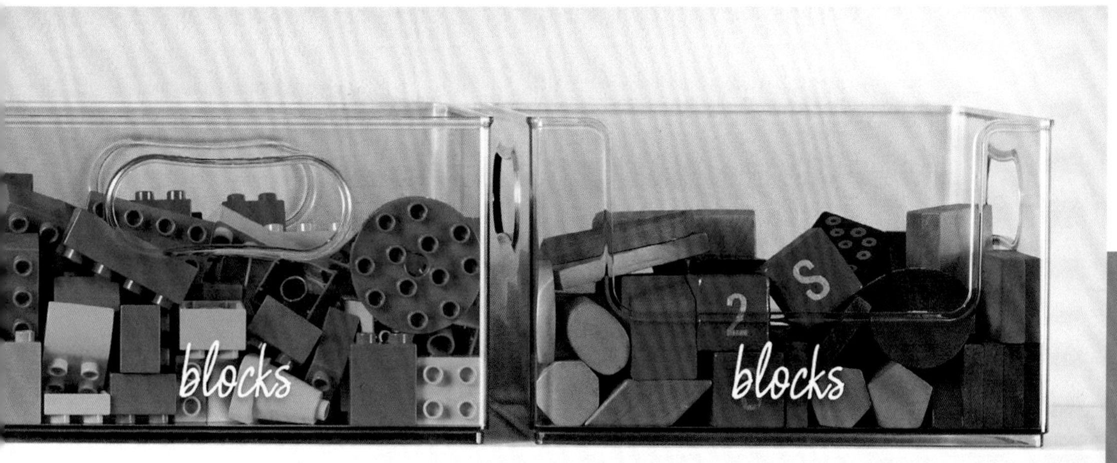

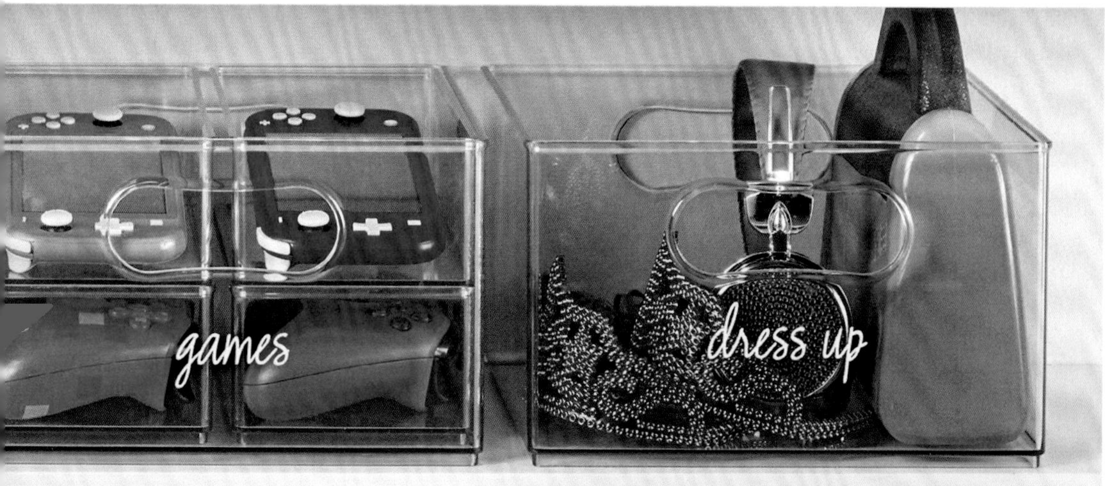

games
dress up

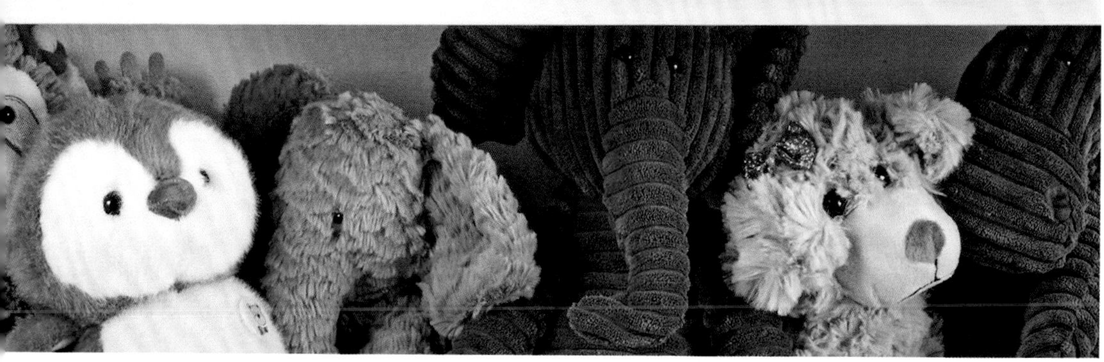

FUNDAMENTALS CHECKLIST FOR KIDS' ZONES

Need to have:

- Hangers, drawers, or bins for clothes
- Bins or baskets for toys
- Homework or schoolwork station
- Storage for sentimental items

Nice to have:

- Donation bin for outgrown clothes and toys no longer in use
- Drawer dividers to keep like with like
- Dedicated shelving for crafts and games
- Out-of-season storage
- Kid-sized robot who won't talk back when asked to clean up and might even make you lunch

MORNING STAR

Don't you just *love* mornings? Spending the first few minutes of the day with your happy family, everyone well rested, smiling, and calm, everyone agreeing on their outfits and a healthy breakfast—

&^%)(*&R#JLGOP*TJ!!!!!

OOPS! Sorry, that was our heads hitting the keyboard as we snapped out of that fantasy. We know as well as you do that mornings are kinda the worst. So what can the maintenance-minded parent do to diminish the pain? Prepare! We set up this system with days-of-the-week bins that can be stocked on the weekend, when it actually is possible that family members are being agreeable. This particular closet is for a little girl, but it can be customized for just about any age child who is willing to exercise their autonomy in clothing choice (with a little bit of adult help when needed). Once they can write, encourage their organizing impulses by having them write their own labels.

NO HARD WIRING

This family had the right impulse for their son's closet, but what they didn't know was that they weren't actually open-wire-bin people. Either you're an open-wire person (meaning someone who is willing to keep everything neatly sorted, folded, and tidy, because the contents will always be clearly on display) or you're not, and sometimes you only find out the hard way. Luckily these bins are versatile enough that they could be put to good use elsewhere in the house.

Baskets that are the correct size, labeled, and don't require perfect folding to work (are the swim trunks in a big jumble? If you can't see them, it doesn't count), allow the top shelf to accommodate books. You know the saying "measure twice, cut once"? We say measure twice, then go buy the baskets that fit your space and you may even gain an entire extra shelf. Shirts are hung in short-sleeve and long-sleeve groupings so there's no fumbling to figure out where something goes, and boots that are worn only occasionally go to the highest shelf, while sneakers get easy-access shelving.

AFTER

HAPPY FEET

There are two kinds of people in the world. The first kind finds folding overwhelming, and the second kind thinks folding is therapeutic. You can guess which camp we fall into! If you're reading this book, there's a good chance folding makes you happy too—but it's *not* for everyone.

If you are person 1, and you don't like to fold, all is not lost. Enter the drawer divider. Either expandable or set inserts, drawer dividers allow you to separate items without actually having to totally deal with them. With this drawer, of course we took the time to fold these adorable socks and onesies, because free therapy. But if you need to just put dividers in your drawers to keep, say, the onesies and socks apart, never fold a thing, and call the whole operation a triumph, that's okay too. Maybe get your therapy someplace else.

BEFORE

AFTER

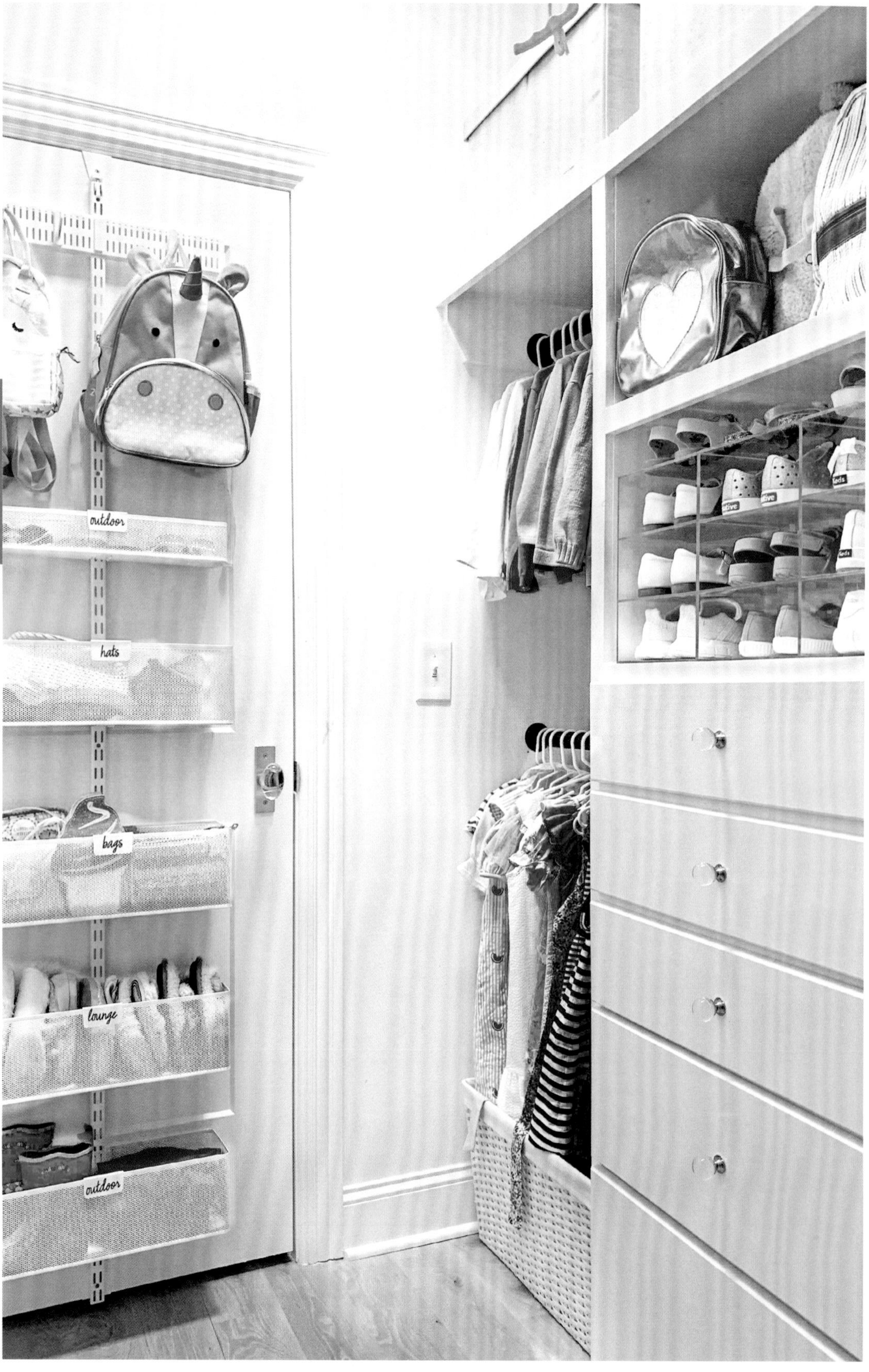
outdoor
hats
bags
lounge
outdoor

THE MAGIC DOOR

Have we introduced you to our friend Elfa? She is so talented and multifunctional. Seriously, for a relatively inexpensive, highly flexible solution, Elfa over-the-door units are the best friend you never knew you needed. All that's required is a door, and we're guessing you have one of those. You can customize this system to work just about anywhere, but for this kid's closet, we used adjustable mesh baskets that make it easy to see what's inside without demanding A+ tidiness. Elfa is also the queen of maintenance; as this child grows, baskets can be rearranged, heights can be adjusted, and hooks can be added as needed.

HARSH BUT EFFECTIVE PHRASES TO GET YOUR KIDS TO MIND THEIR STUFF

Joanna: "If it's on the floor, you must not care about it."
Clea: "This is going into the put-on-notice bin. If you can't put it away, it gets donated after two weeks."

ANYTHING BUT SLIME

It's not that we don't appreciate crafting or people who like to craft—but we're really craft *supply* people. We have been known to spend hours, literally, sorting through colorful baubles, beads, and pom-poms. What could be more fun than color-coordinating crayons, markers, and paint? Just don't ask us to use any of the things we organized.

Before we got our hands on this closet, the family had already invested in lots of bins, but each was just a hodgepodge of arts and crafts. Now each type of craft supply has its own labeled bin, organized by color, with the prettiest items in the clear inserts that we affectionately refer to as "baby bins," or bins within bins (you know we love a category—and baby bins allow us to have *sub-categories*). Messy things like glue and glitter are up higher. Yes, glitter. We struggled through this one. But *at least there was no slime*, which is, and forever shall be, on our No-Fly List.

Little tip for puzzles: Does it drive you crazy that the boxes always fall apart? Same. We like to toss the box and put the pieces in a zippered pouch and attach a photo of the puzzle to the front. Or you can cut off the front of the box and include it in the bag instead. Either way, no more broken boxes.

KIDS' ZONES

Toy Tolerance: ARE YOU A CLEA OR A JOANNA?

For this scale, 0 = high tolerance; 10 = no tolerance

LEGOS

Joanna: 2.5

Clea: 7

Fun fact: *At the age of 5, Joanna's son Miles built Lego sets and sold them to neighborhood kids for a profit. Clearly Clea's Lego resistance has prevented her own son, Sutton, from becoming a Lego entrepreneur.*

DOLLS/DOLL ACCESSORIES

Joanna: 0

Clea: 3 (8.5 on large doll accoutrements, such as the American Girl horse trailer her daughter Stella wanted one year)

Fun fact #1: *The only dolls that can stay in the house forever are the Clea/Joanna Barbie Dolls.*

Fun fact #2: *Joanna actually likes the small pieces that come with American Girl dolls but is aligned with Clea that the bulky items have to go.*

TOYS THAT MAKE NOISE

Joanna and Clea are both 10, and exceptions are made *only* when the child is less than 9 months old.

CRAFT SUPPLIES: MESSY ART

Joanna and Clea: "Not allowed in my house."

NONMESSY ART

Joanna and Clea: "Washable markers only."

Fun fact (or not fun, depending on who you ask): *Clea allows messy art in the garage, but still gives a hard pass on slime, glitter, and sand.*

activity
learning

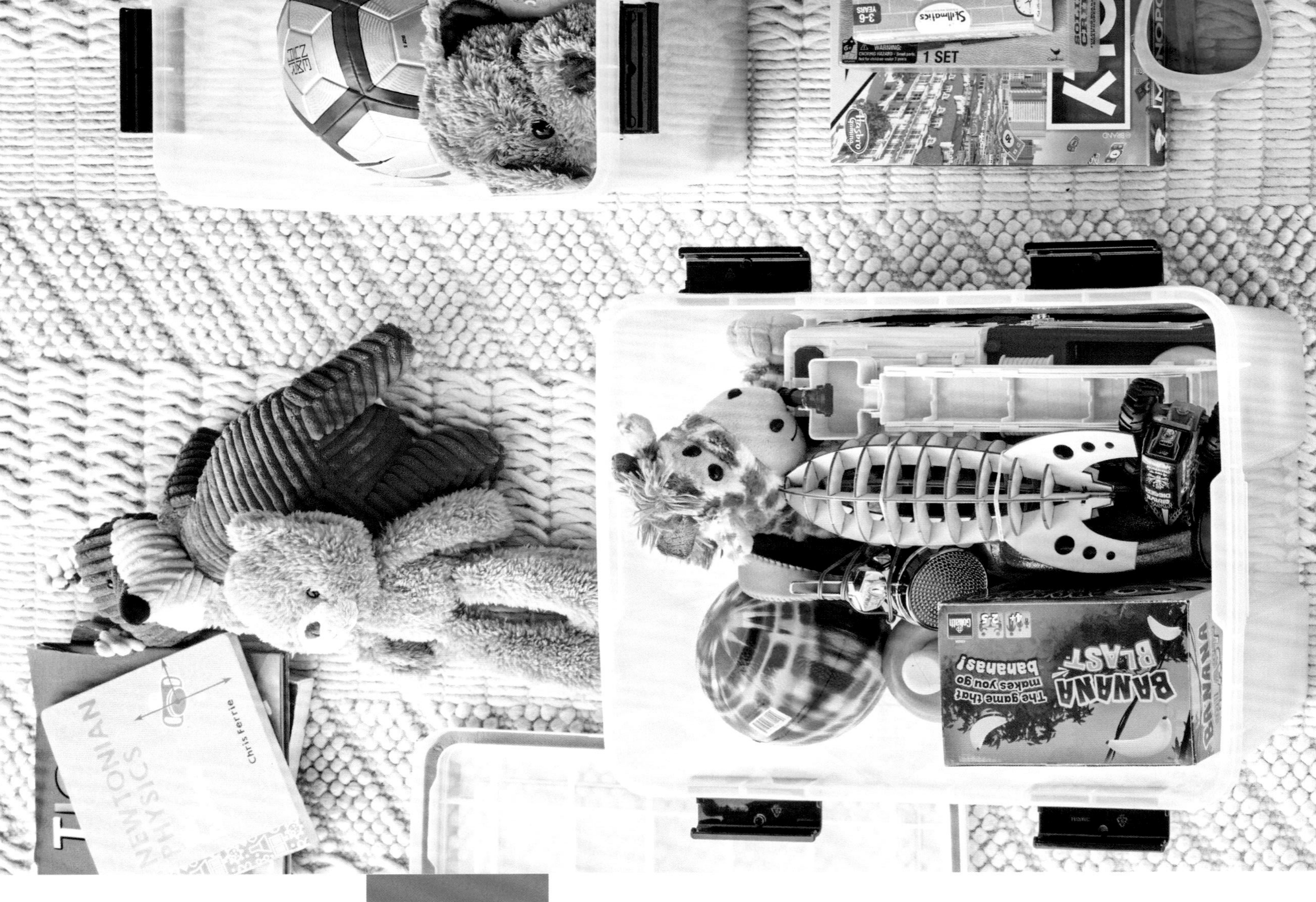
NEWTONIAN PHYSICS
Chris Ferrie
BANANA BLAST
The game that makes you go bananas!
Skillmatics
1 SET
3-6 YEARS

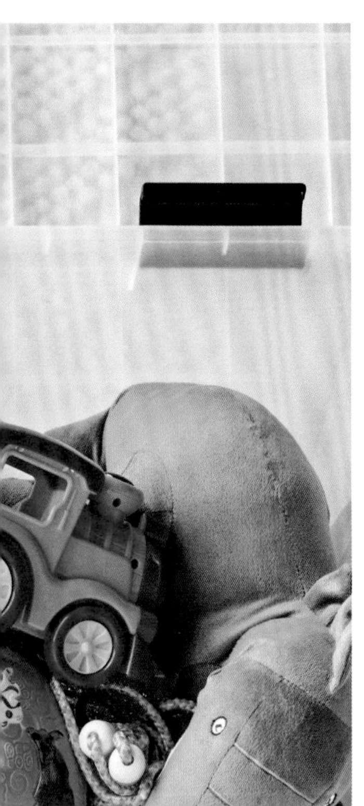

LOW-BAR LIFESTYLE LONG-TERM GOALS

- If it's hard to figure out what to do with kids' school stuff—and it just keeps coming! Every day!: Have a box labeled by grade where you put things you may want to keep. At the end of the school year, revisit what you have and decide if everything is actually worth keeping.

- Keep a box in your child's bedroom for sentimental items; sort through everything when the box is full.

- Keep kids' bedding simple; five throw pillows may look nice on an adult bed, but it looks like a giant stop sign when you ask your kid to make his bed in the morning.

- If your children can't fold, they can put their clothes on hangers. If they can't put their clothes on hangers, they can put them in a bin. Remember: Meeting them where they live is the only hope you have!

HOME OFFICE

DIFFICULTY LEVEL: ★★★★★☆☆☆☆

While we touched on home offices in our previous books, a lot has changed since then. You know . . . unprecedented times and such. Now people are working from home more than ever or living hybrid professional lives, working partly in the office and partly at home. It's a combination that provides a challenge but also moments of magic. Your home office may be a big room with a big desk and supplies at your fingertips, or it may be a cart that you push from the couch to your kitchen table. Regardless, if your schedule means you spend time working at home, remember what they say: With great freedom comes great responsibility. Meaning your WFH, more-flexible existence requires extra effort in the home office organizing and maintenance department.

As we juggle remote and in-person work, we're also trying to navigate the old school/new school divide that we at The Home Edit affectionately refer to as "the Dark Ages vs. the Digital." It's an epic battle, with people who need their paper files in bona fide filing cabinets in one corner and those who prefer digital files on their (virtual) desktops in the other. Most of us in the modern world need to accommodate both, even if some of us lean more dark ages (Joanna) and others more digital (Clea). And like flex work itself, it's the combination of the two that provides the challenge (sometimes) and the magic (*always*).

FIVE MESSY OFFICE EXCUSES, DEBUNKED

1 *"Everybody uses 'my' home office. It's the homework station, the Fantasy Football check-in center, the family accounting office. If I had the room to myself, I could keep it organized."*

Accept your reality. Whether you like it or not, your office is now everyone's office. It helps to designate zones with systems catered to the people using them. Maybe a neatly categorized drawer works for you, but a cart will be much easier for your kids to manage. When you do what's best for both worlds, everyone wins.

2 *"My job requires that I have a laptop, a monitor, a printer/scanner, and about four other things that need plugging in. My desk looks like it took a field trip to an electronics store."*

Bundle them together and conceal them in a box. Not sure what we mean here? Just keep reading.

3 *"Office? What office? Every room in my house is my office. I work at the kitchen counter, store files in my bedroom closet, and take Zoom meetings from the couch."*

And that's completely fine! All that matters is that you designate a space where all your items are going to live when you're not working. Otherwise, it will be harder to mentally "clock in" and "clock out" at the end of the day, which is necessary for our overall well-being.

4 *"My partner calls me a hoarder, but I have a really hard time purging papers in my office. Whether it's family photos or tax returns from 2002, I just worry about throwing things away that I will need or want later."*

DIGITIZE THEM!! That's the beauty of papers . . . you can always scan them and free yourself from that visual clutter. You'll be able to categorize your files into folders, so they are easily searchable.

5 *"Now that I work from home half the time, I have no idea what's at home, what's in my office, and how to keep everything organized in each place."*

First things first, start thinking about your home office and your "office" office as separate entities. Take out a piece of paper (or open your Notes app) and write down what a typical day looks like in each of these spaces. What items do you need to do your job effectively? Are there any tasks you tackle in one office but not the other? Then create systems accordingly.

FUNDAMENTALS CHECKLIST FOR ANY HOME OFFICE

Need to have:

- Storage system for important paperwork
- Charging solution for digital devices
- Clutter-free workspace
- Storage for small items (pens, notepads, scissors, staplers, etc.)

Nice to have:

- Docking station for digital devices
- Closed-door storage for items not in use
- Color-coded filing system for different subjects and family members
- Ties or clips to keep cords in check
- Fresh flowers
- Peace and quiet *(we're not asking for much here!)*

OPEN WIDE

This spectacular setup is gorgeous, aspirational, and an *absolute no-go* for people who aren't willing to do daily (or at least weekly) maintenance. Our client wanted to bring more functionality to their open shelving, and we were more than happy to oblige, as long as they agreed to have a dedicated space for less attractive items and things they didn't want to look at every day, which we put in the labeled baskets. Otherwise, this office is a study in organized accessibility, with key supplies in easy-access letter trays and dividers (clear plastic makes it easy to see when you are running low). Boxes with lids are great for things that either shouldn't get dusty or aren't frequently used—plus they are beautiful, and still in reach when needed.

As for desks, if yours is on the smaller side, like this one, you need to be realistic about what you're going to keep on top of it. Here, we were able to keep the desktop free by putting the shelves to good use (even the pens found a home there!). If you don't have a big desktop or hardworking shelves, keeping a cart nearby with all your essentials can be just as efficient.

LOVE
ORSAY
CHANEL

inbox
outbox
school
sentimental
kids
medical
home
taxes

FAMILY-FRIENDLY FILING

Have we mentioned that it's impossible to underestimate the power of the hanging file? This setup is perfect for a family where any number of people need to access items in the "office," or, in this case, the faux office (fauffice? Did we just make up a new word?), which is where they keep documents and paper.

Ugh, paper. We've visited countless houses where clients have set up filing systems with every intention of maintaining them, but somehow the paper piles prevail. We're here to tell you that *filing is not an impossible task*. You just need (a) space, (b) sufficient hanging files, (c) clear labels, and (d) a small investment of time.

Do you know the "touch it once" rule? Well, you should. Here's how it goes:

Pick it up, look it over, and don't just put it down—put it where it belongs.

It's that easy!

This ROYGBIV filing system is tailored to the "touch it once" rule, so kids and spouses and anybody will understand where things belong. The best part: You don't need a just-right undercounter area for file boxes like these. They can go on a shelf in a closet, in the garage, or even travel with you to the couch if you want to file while you binge-watch something. And if you have to spend time filing, that sounds pretty good.

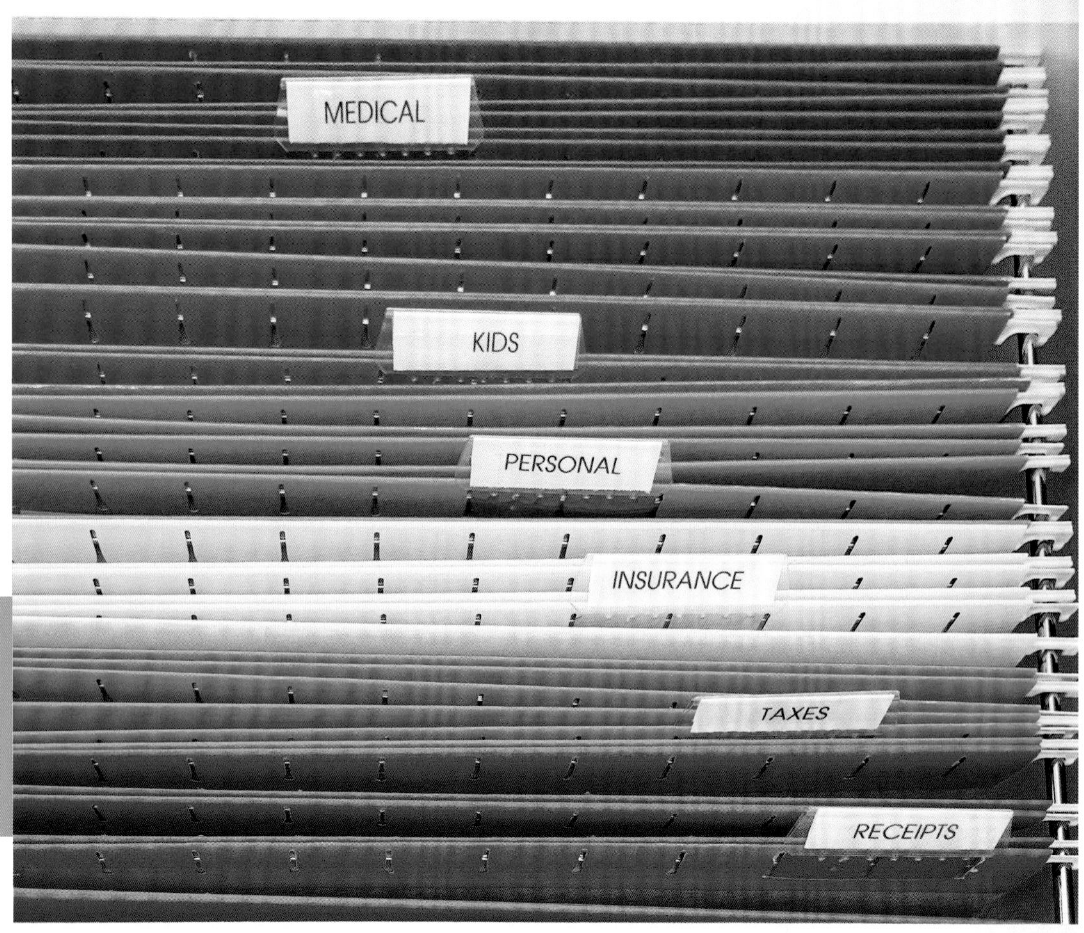

COMMON PAPER CATEGORIES*

GENERAL

- Auto
- Home
- Finances
- Medical
- Important documents
- Education
- Kids

SPECIFIC

- Insurance
- Receipts
- Taxes
- Personal

*Use separate folders for each family member's documents as necessary.

Just Google It: FIVE THINGS YOU CAN GET RID OF IMMEDIATELY BECAUSE OF THE INTERNET

1. Instruction manuals

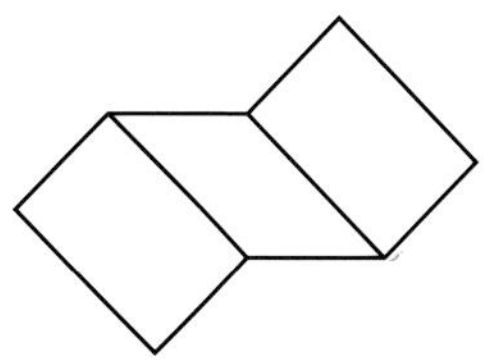

2. Maps

3. Bank statements

4. Insurance benefits

5. Warranties

OUR HERO, THE HUMBLE CART

Rolling charging station on wheels, we love you for so many reasons and here's why:

1. You're flexible! You travel easily from room to room.
2. You help us contain some of the least beautiful items necessary for modern living (looking at you, cords).
3. You prevent the members of our families from having to sift through drawers or dig through backpacks (and leave a mess!).
4. You sneakily encourage family time! As in, "Let's all put our devices in the cart and make eye contact!"
5. You provide storage and charging, all in one.
6. You allow us to keep track of all the bits and parts that come with phones, laptops, headphones, iPads, and the like.

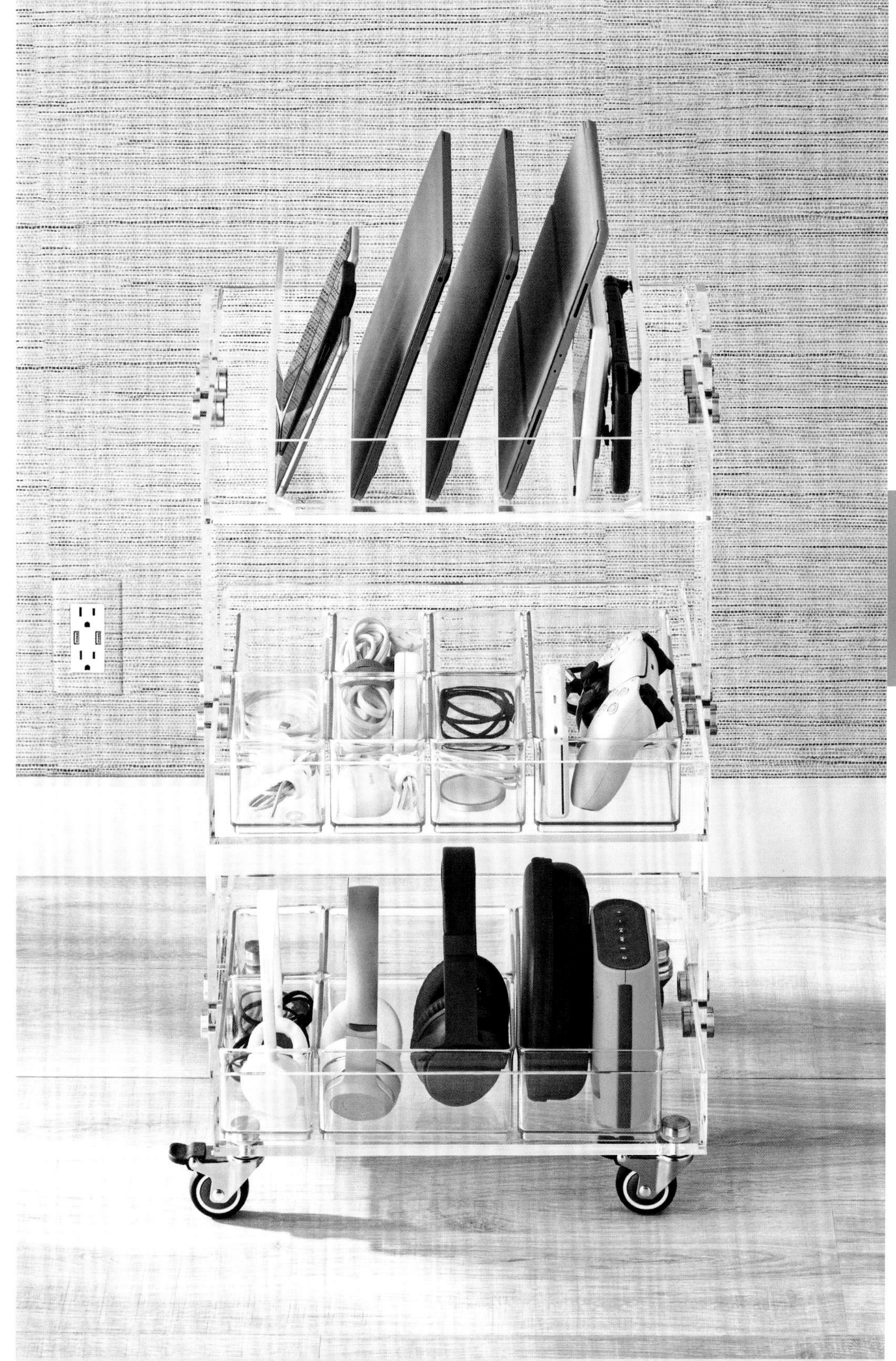

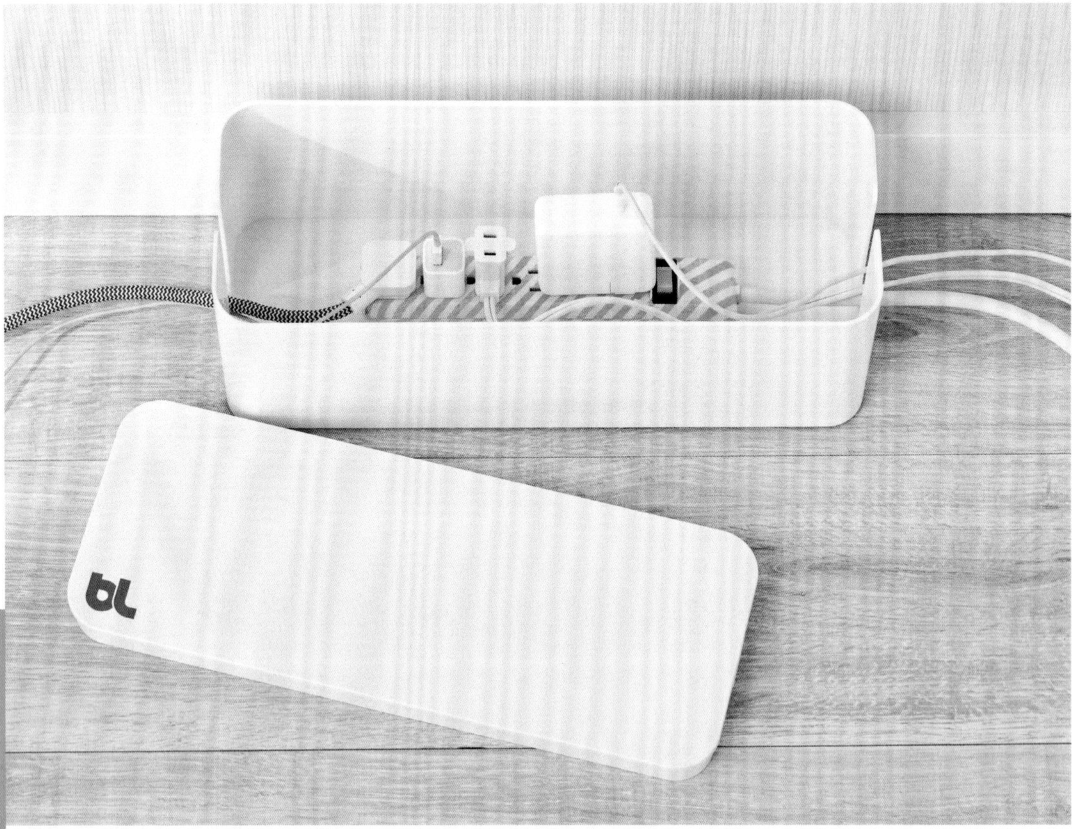

printer
phone
watch
ipad
laptop
lamp

PLUG AND PLAY

It was a sad day when we realized that there was *simply no way* we could completely eliminate cords from our lives. There are so many things to hate about cords: They tangle, they're not attractive while plugged in, and not attractive when they're tucked away. They are necessary but unruly. And for the foreseeable future, it seems like some cords are here to stay. Which is why we also know about these things, the greatest hits of cord maintenance:

1. THE CABLE ZIPPER

What it is: a long tube that you wrap around cables
Good for: corralling multiple cords all headed to the same place

2. CABLE DROP CLIPS

What they are: cute little bagel- or donut-looking things
Good for: holding your phone charger in place

3. CABLE LABELS

What they are: exactly what they sound like
Good for: knowing the difference between the cord that plugs into your laptop and the one that plugs into your phone!

4. CABLE BOX (not that kind)

What it is: genius rectangular box to hide an ugly power strip on the floor or desktop
Good for: condensing cord volume; improved happiness

5. SILICONE TIES

What they are: ties that come in every color to keep cords tangle-free
Good for: bundling smaller cords (headphones, phone chargers) so they are easy to find and easy to travel with

HOW WE WORK FROM HOME

SPACE

Clea: my dining room table
Joanna: my upstairs office

OUTFIT

Clea: jeans and a sweater
Joanna: cute sweater and leggings

MUST-HAVE OFFICE ITEMS

Clea: phone, AirPods, beverage of choice
Joanna: half-caf almond milk latte, headband, Poppin pens (my favorite!)

PRODUCTIVITY HACK

Clea: turn on Do Not Disturb on my phone
Joanna: schedule ten-minute walk breaks throughout the day

BIGGEST DISTRACTION

Clea: the number of texts always coming in
Joanna: my brain

SNACK BREAK

Clea: salt and vinegar pistachios
Joanna: walk in to the pantry for nuts but end up leaving with candy

supplies
planners
cricut
cricut
paper

BEFORE

AFTER

FUN WITHIN REASON

This client's desk told us a lot about her, meaning that she's definitely a *drawer person*. If you're tempted, as she was, to keep things on the surface of your desk, first ask yourself: Am I the type of person who is going to maintain this? Or am I a drawer person? We're not saying one is better than the other (after all, sometimes artfully displaying things on surfaces keeps you from adding things that don't belong there), but you need to understand which desk approach suits your personality—aka your fussy factor.

And now look who has her desk back!! To ensure the system would be easy to maintain, we designated strategic zones. The drawers to the far right and far left hold items she uses daily—think glasses and scissors. In the middle two drawers (which are harder to access when she's sitting at the desk) are stationery and other paper goods that she uses only on occasion. Always remember to follow the path of least resistance. When items are easy to grab, they'll be easy to put away.

Btw . . . you didn't think we were just going to skip over the wallpaper, did you?! Just because a place is for work doesn't mean it has to be sterile or boring. If you fill your workspace with colors and things that make you happy (the red trays on the desk really spoke to this client), spending a few minutes a week on maintenance won't feel like as much of a chore.

PINKY SWEAR

Honestly, we think we could write a whole book about the desk chair in this client's home office. Now, *that* is a desk chair. As anyone who operates a company out of a small space (in this case, an apartment) can tell you, maintaining tight organization is crucial to peace of mind, not to mention business success. This client runs a fashion brand and needs a space that's inspiring, not stuffy, where work and home can live together in harmony. Wire-mesh drawers maintain office essentials, while the desktop stays neat with just the things she uses throughout the day. Oversize, clear plastic bins hold stock above the open rack, while tissue and other paper goods stay organized in flat bins beneath the clothes. The whole thing feels a bit like a retail store—functional and fun.

HOW TO CONTROL YOUR EMAIL INBOX . . . BEFORE IT CONTROLS YOU

If staying on top of your email feels like an uphill battle, that's because it is. We recently read somewhere that the average person receives up to one hundred emails a day. YES . . . ONE HUNDRED. With all the other things on our to-do list, striving for Inbox Zero on a daily basis is an unrealistic endeavor. Instead, here are some ways to beat the system and create your own:

- Allocate a specific time of day to check your email.
- For every email you receive, use one of the 4 D's (do, delete, delegate, or defer) . . . then *delete some more*. Seriously, delete as many as you can.
- Turn off notifications for new emails (too distracting) as well as all social media notifications (way too many!).
- Turn on your email preview feature; it will enable you to delete some emails without fully "reading" them.
- Create labels and folders to sort emails you need to keep.
- Set aside a time once a month to unsubscribe to all unwanted emails.
- Set up filters for incoming email.
- Create a new email address for promotions and another one for online orders and receipts.
- Touch it once! (Yes, this can apply to the digital world, too.)
- Star or flag important emails that you can't deal with immediately.

23
24
25
023/342
024/341
025/340
30
31
030/335
031/334
January
February

THE SELF-CLEANING DESK

And now, for the little containment system that could. Sometimes all you need in life to make you feel like you've really got it together is a pretty setup on your desk for the things you grab all day long. (Are we saying you could replace those pushpins with Swedish Fish? 100 percent.) Whether you are a surface person or a drawer person, whether you work at a desk or your dining room table, a functional tray or system of small bins that holds your "touch access" essentials can travel with you. Know that every time you put those scissors or a pen back where it belongs, you are maintaining your system. And you can do it *all day long*. Gold star for you!

LOW-BAR LIFESTYLE LONG-TERM GOALS

- If your office is now everyone's office, accept your reality and designate zones and systems that are catered to the people using them.
- Follow the "touch it once" rule: Pick it up, look it over, file it away.
- Dedicate five minutes at the end of every workday to put things back where they belong.
- Extra low-bar lifestyle goal: If you must bring your work items home with you, designate a visible zone for them so nothing gets lost in the mix.

CLOSET

DIFFICULTY LEVEL: ★★★★★★☆☆☆

There is something mysteriously satisfying about having an organized closet. Unlike many spaces in your home, your bedroom closet doesn't get a lot of exposure. It's not like the entry, where friends and strangers alike can wander in and judge your organizing skills. Or your kitchen (which surely contains a magnet since everyone gravitates and clusters), opening all your cabinets and drawers in search of the garbage can. No, your bedroom closet gets very little action from anyone who doesn't already know and love you, meaning nobody is going to judge you based solely on whether the space is perfectly neat or in complete shambles.

But . . . when you open a closet door to find a beautifully maintained space—shoes lined up in pairs, clothes draped gracefully on hangers, bins lining a shelf—it's like your own little secret victory. Nobody needs to see it for you to know it's there (even though showing off all your hard work feels pretty great, too!). When you keep your closet in line, you have arrived at organizational nirvana. Do you ever lie in bed after a tough day, feeling anxious, thoughts scrambling all over the place, then think about your neatly arranged closet and feel your mind and body relax? Because we do . . . and we *know* we're not the only ones. That's the power of an organized closet, y'all.

But getting there and staying there both require effort on your end. After all, most closets have doors. And you know what doors mean: The toss-it-in-there-and-deal-with-it-later risk is dangerously high. Life gets busy, the days are rushed, and what's the harm of just throwing those cute rainbow sneakers on the floor instead of putting them back where they belong? Well, it's like an avalanche: One little slip becomes a messy, heavy, swirling pile, and those cute rainbow sneakers may never be seen again.

We're here to help keep you on track. To remind you that maintaining organization in a space that random acquaintances will never see can feel like the biggest win of all. No one may know that your sweaters are neatly folded, your shoes are in lidded bins, and all of your hangers match. But you know. And that's all that matters.

FIVE MESSY CLOSET EXCUSES, DEBUNKED

1 *"I don't have a lot of clothes, but I live in a tiny apartment and my bedroom has the smallest closet in the world, so I have piles of shirts, pants, and shoes all over my room."*

Even the smallest closets have storage opportunities. You just need to look up, look down, and turn yourself around *(wait, did we just invent our first viral TikTok dance?)* to notice them. Door, floor, and top-shelf storage is valuable real estate with the right solutions, so go find it!

2 *"I have a walk-in closet, but I share it with my husband. We've managed to divide the space, but his side is a gigantic mess, and it pains me to look at it."*

At this point, "In separate closets or shared" should be a part of wedding vows. It's important to realize that just because a system works for you doesn't mean it will work for your husband. Everyone has a different fussy factor, routine, and items to account for.

3 *"I make good use of the shelves in my closet, although everything is always falling over. I start with neat piles and after a couple of weeks you'd never know I folded anything."*

Some items lack structural integrity. It's really not your fault. At the end of the day, a cashmere sweater is going to do what a cashmere sweater is going to do. We reference this frustrating fact of life on page 169 of this chapter. We know you'll probably skip straight there, but make sure to come right back. You won't want to miss all the helpful topics we cover on the way!

4 *"I want to have the kind of closet I see on Instagram! How do I get there if I can't afford to spend the money on the matching hangers, boxes, and bins that it would require?"*

Organization isn't all or nothing. It's not go big or go home. It's a journey you will always gain something from, even if you start small or without any product. Something as simple as creating a denim bar (aka folded jeans stacked on a shelf) can transform the way you interact with your closet daily.

5 *"Sorting my clothes in ROYGBIV order doesn't work for me—everything I have is black, or a print. So how do I come up with a smart system?"*

We've literally had people ask us if they need to own clothing in every color in order for us to organize their closet. And the answer is no! The ROYGBIV method is just sorting your clothes in the order of the rainbow spectrum. Skip over the colors you don't see. But there are also sorting methods that have little to do with color. Stay tuned, we touch on that shortly.

THE FUNDAMENTALS CHECKLIST FOR A CLOSET

Need to have:

- Hanging system for clothes that need to be hung
- Bins or drawers for clothes that need to be folded
- Storage for shoes
- Storage for other accessories (belts, jewelry, purses)

Nice to have:

- Shelf dividers
- Shallow drawers with dividers for jewelry
- Rotation space for seasonal storage
- Open shelving to display your favorite items
- Life coach, therapist, or best friend to call as you try on those jeans that haven't fit since 2014

COLOR GUARD

If you've followed our work over the years, even with only one eye open—*even then* you'll know that rainbows are our thing. We personally find rainbows fun and visually appealing, but they also create a logical way of sorting your items. Some people ROYGBIV (yes, we've made it a verb) their whole closet; some ROYGBIV within certain categories (tanks vs. jackets vs. dresses).

But we know that not everyone lives in a ROYGBIV world, and so we get a lot of questions. Most along these lines: What happens if my clothes don't form a rainbow? Do I just *live in chaos?!?!*

First, know that we would never suggest you set up and attempt to maintain a system that will stress you out. What we hope to offer is the opposite of stress. The rainbow is a labeling mechanism, but if that isn't the one that works for you, then you need to find a solution that does.

As with so many things in life, the answer lies with . . . the Ouija board. Okay, most things don't tie back to a Ouija board, but it's helpful to think about in this case. Remember how you play the Ouija board? You let the planchette (which is the piece you move along the board, and no, we didn't know that's what it's called either) guide you to the right answer. Similarly, you need to let your clothes guide you to where they want to live. (Even if you don't ROYGBIV, this works especially well for clothes with plaids and prints.) Take an item and try it in a few different spots. Trust us, you will know where it belongs when it looks and feels right to you.

Gettysvue
shoes
shoes
shoes
shoes
shoes
boots
boots

NEGATIVE FEEDBACK

Before we get into why we're majorly obsessed with using negative space, let's talk about how we begin any closet organizing job, whether for a client or in our own homes. It boils down to three questions:

1. What do you need to store?
2. Where are the opportunities/where can stuff go?
3. What containment system works for these items and how do you use them?

Sounds easy and easy to maintain. But when a system begins to break down, it's often due to a failure of negative space—meaning the unused areas that are just begging to be put to work. Take Clea's closet. Her tops, sweaters, jeans, and shoes all have very specific places to live. But beneath her clothes there was empty space that desperately needed a job. She made great use of it with a The Home Edit bag and lidded boxes to hold jewelry, watches, and sunglasses.

So, ask yourself: **What do I need to store? Is there negative space I can take advantage of? If so, all it requires is the right storage system.**

THE

school

TAKE THE FLOOR

You don't need us to point out that this organizing system is a triumph in the use of negative space. Lots and lots of sweaters + a nook beneath the shelves that is perfect for stacking = a beautiful marriage. The sweaters are lovely, but really, there's nothing under the sun more lovely than creating storage where storage didn't exist before.

You'll notice that in this bedroom, there is not a hanger in sight. Some people just are bin people, and that's fine by us (the bin inclination—*binclination!*—runs strong in Joanna's gene pool). As you are maintaining your closet, and constantly assessing the best use of your space, pay attention to whether it's easier to keep things folded, hung up, at eye level, hidden, or out in the open. (Not everyone would be able to pull off this stacked sweater scenario–*and that's okay*.) For the most part, folding takes more time than hanging, but for those of us who are "under tall" (ahem, Joanna), hanging things on high bars may be a nonstarter.

Your path of least resistance is most likely the system you are going to maintain. It's not any more complicated than that.

SHIRT FOLDING TUTORIAL

1 Lay the shirt on any flat surface (see page 65). Smooth out any wrinkles. Fold over the left and right sleeves.

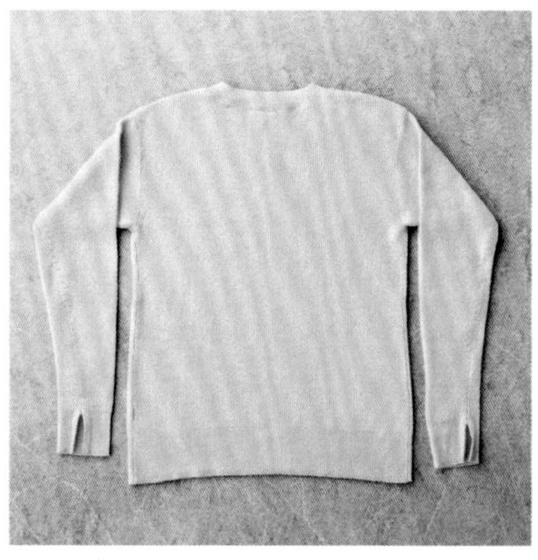

2 Fold the left sleeve back toward the shirt hem.

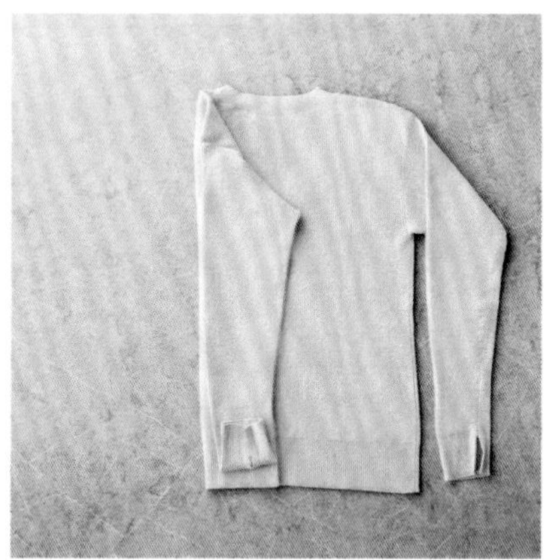

3 Fold the right sleeve back toward the shirt hem.

4 Fold the bottom up toward the center.

5 Fold the top down over the bottom.

6 Turn the shirt around. Done!

CLOSET

BACK TO BASICS

When you invest in key foundational pieces that mix and match, you can build multiple outfits that stand the test of time. Aka your capsule wardrobe! It's like a school uniform for adults. You'll never feel panicked that you have nothing to wear! Here's an example checklist as reference:

Tops

- [ ] Camisole tank
- [ ] Basic white T-shirt
- [ ] Fun graphic T-shirt
- [ ] Solid color shirt
- [ ] Striped or patterned shirt
- [ ] Long-sleeve shirt
- [ ] Basic white button-down
- [ ] Denim/chambray button-down
- [ ] Crewneck sweater
- [ ] Cozy sweatshirt
- [ ] Turtleneck

Bottoms

- [ ] Comfortable jeans
- [ ] Tailored trousers
- [ ] Wide-leg pants
- [ ] Leggings
- [ ] Pencil skirt

Jackets

- [ ] Trench coat
- [ ] Leather jacket
- [ ] Denim jacket
- [ ] Blazer
- [ ] Cardigan

Dresses

- [ ] Black cocktail dress
- [ ] Patterned dress

Shoes

- [ ] White sneakers
- [ ] Loafers or flats
- [ ] Ankle boots
- [ ] Neutral heels
- [ ] Sandals

Accessories

- [ ] Everyday tote bag
- [ ] Crossbody (or chic fanny pack!)
- [ ] Clutch
- [ ] Black or brown belt
- [ ] Linen scarf
- [ ] Wool or knit scarf
- [ ] And most importantly . . . A HEADBAND *(OR 50 OF THEM)*

FROM MIXED TO MATCHED

This client had a good closet, but it needed a little face-lift to reenergize the space. As you can see, the husband and wife share the space equally, which in a lot of homes feels unfair to begin with. (Clea would *even cook dinner* for her husband if he'd give up some of his space in their shared closet—see page 170 for details. And if you fully understand how little Clea cooks, you know what a sacrifice that would be.) In this closet, the wife's side is too packed (we dare you to count the hangers), there's no consistency of clothing arrangement, and the upper shelves are full of random stuff. The negative space is being utilized—we guess? But if you can explain the reasoning behind what goes where, please get in touch asap.

AFTER

BEFORE

AFTER

If you've been counting the hangers in the before photo, you can stop. The number stayed the same. So, what's different?

We've helped take advantage of every bit of space. Gone is the mixed salad of hangers—now everything is hung on slim wood or slim huggable velvet hangers (our personal go-tos). Clothing items have found their zones, and the shoes are organized by the "touch access" requirement: Everyday shoes with a low profile now live in an easy-access spot beneath the hanging clothes, while dressier shoes that are worn less often are on the top shelf in closed storage. Labeled bins hold seldom-used or off-season items, while wire baskets with individual inserts hold smaller items such as phone chargers and AirPods that need to stay in the closet but don't need to be kept in sight.

IF THE SHOE FITS . . .

. . . you might want to put it in a bin. If it doesn't fit in a bin, try it on a shelf. If it doesn't fit on a shelf, find a way to use the negative space under your clothes. In other words: You can *always* find a spot for your shoes; you might just have to dig a little.

If you are lucky enough to have the luxury of *choosing* a shoe system, then you have the freedom to follow your preference. Again, ask yourself which is the path of least resistance for you. Our MVPs:

- **Lidded storage:** Relatively inexpensive, and great for moving things around and keeping dust out, but it requires an extra step to access your shoes (not a complicated step but still a step!).
- **Drop-front shoe storage:** Stackable, so this allows you to double or even triple your shoe storage. It also provides easier access than lidded storage while still keeping your shoes dust-free and protected. But stackable storage can be a nonstarter with high heels.

- **Open stacking:** The hybrid solution between lidded or drop-front storage and open shelves, this is a great solution if you want immediate access to your shoes and like the enforced structure of individual slots.
- **Open shelves:** Makes for easy access and low-effort organizing, but the shelves need to be the right height for your shoes. You're at the mercy of your space in a way that won't work for some.

We're often asked which direction people should face their shoes. The only answer is that consistency is key. But you can have a little fun from shelf to shelf. Clea sets up her shoes based on which way they look best, and then faces every pair on the shelf in the same direction. Ouija-board style, she lets her shoes reveal their best angle. When the shoes look happy, Clea's happy.

AT THE READY

This client's closet is a great example of what happens when you hunt for any space available and utilize it as best as possible. Because she had a lot of bulky necklaces and limited shelf space, we used a rod with individual hooks to keep them separate but easy to grab, with a mirror and ottoman to help make this her get-ready area. On the shelf, more delicate necklaces and bracelets are organized by frequency of use—with subcategories contained in baby bins—and her hamper fits neatly underneath.

THE HOME EDIT GO BAG

Core principles: being ready so you don't have to get ready, traveling light isn't a thing, and using separate zippered pouches for all your categories

CLEA

- Low-carb tortillas, aka "purse tortillas"
- Pistachios
- Phone charger
- Backup phone charger *(you can never be too careful)*
- Kindle
- Spare contacts
- Reading glasses
- Medications
- Hand sanitizer

JOANNA

- Swedish Fish
- Protein bars
- Protein shake
- Reading glasses
- Hand sanitizer
- Day planner
- Spare scarf

TAKE IT TO GO

If you thought stations were just for trains and big wedding reception buffets . . . think again. Sometimes, when confronted with a challenging closet, we will look at each other and don't even need to say a word, because we are thinking the exact same thing: *stations*. It's our own form of mental telepathy, and while it may seem odd to some, it saves us a lot of time!

This closet is a fantastic example of grab-and-go systems at work. Some people have a mudroom, some people have a hall closet or piece of furniture next to the front door. This client has her bedroom. All the major players are here: Labeled bins supplement drawer space, shelf dividers keep clothes in place, slim hangers make the most of the rod space. But it's the use of the door that's the real star, with her sunglasses, hat, and prepacked tote bag with obvious homes and always at the ready. This system is a no-brainer to maintain and requires no additional stops between the bedroom and the front door. Genius.

Oh, and those bins and hooks you see on the door? They are adhesive, removable, and extremely affordable. It's a great vertical solution in any space but especially in a closet where you may need to test out different variations or adjust the positioning as time goes on.

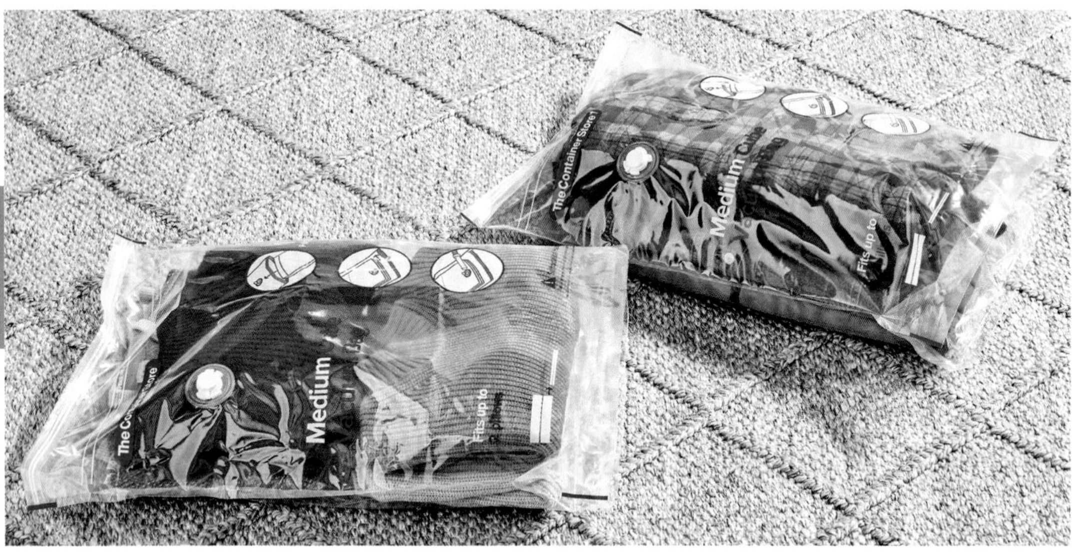

The Container Store
Medium Cube
Fits up to
Medium
Fits up to

Medium Cube
seasonal

BYE FOR NOW

Sometimes even your clothes need a little time-out. If you live in a part of the world with seasons, chances are you've got some sort of system to periodically rotate what you need when you need it. (If you don't have a full closet for off-season clothes, a dedicated section of your closet will do.) For seasonal rotation, there are a few guidelines to keep in mind:

1. If all seasons share the same closet, make front-facing bins the prime real estate for in-use items.

2. Doing a seasonal swap is the perfect time to do a quick pass through your stuff, to give everything the Love vs. Need Litmus Test. Just because you wore something last year doesn't mean you will wear it this year—prime real estate should go only to the things you're really going to use. (And luckily, purging seasonal items tends to be less emotionally fraught than purging clothes; unlike pants, for instance, those mittens are most likely *always* going to fit.)

3. Vacuum storage bags are another space-efficient way to keep your off-season clothing organized and protected.

The Sort Wars: COLOR VS. CATEGORY

Here at The Home Edit, we have a dedicated team of people who are smart, creative, hardworking, and nearly as crazy as we are. We share a mission, and so we're all working toward the same goal. Still, we don't always agree on the answers to some of life's most important questions, such as, Should you organize your clothes by color or by category?

To help us weigh the options, we invited some special guest stars to the chapter, Shaina and Sumner. If you watched our Netflix show, you definitely know them! We will caveat their opinions by saying that, when they work on a client's home, these two always do what's best for the client, choosing the method that suits the client's space and preferences. But in their own closets, they simply do not agree.

SHAINA, ON WHY SHE ORGANIZES BY COLOR

"I'm a visual person, so I may walk into my closet and think, 'I feel like wearing red today.' *For me, color takes priority over categories any day of the week. I've found that this method works best for people who have a specific color in mind in the morning, or those who want their closets to look as boutiquey and ROYGBIV as possible. That is not to say that you should hang your formal dresses next to your sweatpants. I like to give each color a zone, and then group things into broad categories (all the red shirts together, for example) within the zone."*

SUMNER, ON WHY SHE ORGANIZES BY CATEGORY

"So . . . I live solidly in reality, meaning I navigate my closet according to the current temperature outside. *For example, I think, 'Oh, it's seventy degrees. Therefore, I can wear a short-sleeve shirt and jeans, so let me look at all my short-sleeve shirts and see which one is speaking to me.' And I hang all my short-sleeved shirts together, no matter what color they are. Yes, the end result is choppier looking, but it's utilitarian and better for me."*

Who's right? Both of them! But now it's up to you to decide what works best for *you*.

SUPPORT SYSTEM

We're talking shelf dividers, people. If your closet can accommodate them, clear plastic shelf dividers are the load-bearing walls of closets—in other words, absolutely key for structural integrity and general peace of mind.

You know we love sweaters (particularly what we call our "Care Bear Sweaters"—i.e., anything that has an emoji: hearts, stars, rainbows, lightning bolts, you name it). Depending on where you live, you may love sweaters, too. But sweaters can be a closet nightmare. They are unruly, they don't play nice, and they tend to collapse on one another as time goes on—like your friends after a long night at a bar. Which is why shelf dividers are the answer: They help maintain decorum and keep everybody in line.

But it's not just sweaters that can be a problem. Unstructured purses collapse. Tall boots collapse. Tote bags, too. Basically, anything soft or loose or without a base can just get too tired to stand up after a while . . . which, *same*! But we also know that, where maintenance is concerned, shelf dividers can prop everybody up. Including you.

ONE FOR YOU, TWO FOR ME?

Let's just get this out of the way at the beginning: The fact that Clea allows her husband, John, any space whatsoever in this perfect jewel of a closet is basically a humanitarian act. And to further demonstrate her generous spirit, she has agreed to answer three questions:

Does John wear shoes? Because these all look like they belong to you.

Yes! Hahaha, of course he has shoes! You can't see them in the photo, but they are to the right of the door.

Do you organize John's drawers?

No. It's a lawless land that I want no part of.

But do you rehang any of John's clothes because you don't like the way he did it?

Guilty. When pants and jeans are folded the wrong way on a hanger, it makes me start to sweat, and I must fix them immediately. Have I told him how to hang a pair of pants a million times (back seam faces out, front seam faces in)? Yes, but if this is our one major marital breakdown, I'll take it.

Sharing a closet, as we saw on pages 170–71, is a challenge to your space and to your relationship. In order to have a closet that you can both maintain, you need to firmly establish who gets what space at the outset. If anybody breaches the other's space, you need to pull out your relationship bargaining chips, which vary by couple and involve rules of engagement so elaborate that we could write a whole book about it.

In Clea's closet, of course all of our core closet principles are on display (literally): frequently used items given easiest access; clothing separated by category, then ROYGBIV-ed; negative space properly utilized; things Clea loves behind glass doors as pretty focal points that just make her happy; loosey-goosey items that just do not look good, no matter how organized they are (bras, underwear, socks) safely tucked into drawers; and most importantly, no wire hangers in sight.

In a shared closet, kindness must prevail. Clea's kindness to John—in allowing him to keep his clothes here as opposed to, say, the guest room—makes her feel like a pretty decent person. His clothes have seen the inside of a guest room closet once or twice, so this is an upgrade!

See? Maintenance in a properly set up shared closet could not be easier. You wear something, you put it back where you got it. And as long as the other person abides by the "no wire hangers allowed" rule, it's smooth sailing.

LOW-BAR LIFESTYLE LONG-TERM GOALS

- Investing in matching hangers is one of the best ways to elevate the look of your closet and save space on a hanging rack. We cannot recommend this simple switch enough.

- If you feel overwhelmed, commit to one small section that makes you happy, not what needs the most work.

- Whenever you remove an article of clothing from a hanging rod, put the empty hanger back at the same end of the rod each time. Don't just leave it hidden between the rest of your clothes. This simple system will instantly streamline your laundry routine.

KITCHEN

DIFFICULTY LEVEL: ★★★★★★★☆☆

Now, of course, we find ourselves in the kitchen. And the thing about the kitchen is that everything ends up there. No matter how hard you try to avoid it, everything from packages and art projects to sneakers and dog leashes finds its way there. When it comes to the kitchen, we can't even blame our kids for the clutter. We are all guilty of dropping mail on the counter or kicking off our shoes without putting them away. And if you have an extremely naughty puppy (ahem, named Indie Shearer), you also discover things from all over the house that he has helpfully brought into the kitchen, too. We were looking for that one rain boot and an Apple watch charger!

And have you noticed that a kitchen doesn't fill up with just things but also with people? Whether you have two or ten people in your house, they are magnetically tied to the kitchen. You could throw a party with a full bar, a giant cheese board, and a magic show with a live rabbit in your living room—everybody still ends up in the kitchen.

As you can see, a kitchen becomes Grand Central Station on any given day. It's not just a place to cook food (thank goodness, because we're not great at it) but, in fact, the kitchen is a mixed-bag space that tends to tilt toward chaos . . . aka a scary domestic black hole that sucks everything else into it. Is there an alternative, you ask? A foolproof recipe for the perfect, organized kitchen? Of course! Here it is:

Take one normal-sized adult human.

Combine with complete solitude.

Add the absence of hobbies, a job, or the need to eat.

Stir gently.

Voilà! The perfect, organized kitchen.

If, however, you lack the ingredients for that recipe—as most of us do—we're here to propose some alternatives to manage the chaos and navigate the black hole.

FIVE MESSY KITCHEN EXCUSES, DEBUNKED

1 *"I am pretty good at keeping things neat, but my family definitely isn't. They leave their dishes in the sink and the trash can is always overflowing. If I organize the kitchen, it all falls apart within half an hour."*

This is one of the most common excuses in any space: I live with monsters, so what's the point of trying? It all comes down to how you approach the situation. See past the frustration and look for reasonable solutions that will still hold your family accountable. Bribes also go a long way.

2 *"I bake a lot, and don't have pantry space for all the ingredients I use. So I end up just leaving stuff out on the counter, which looks bad and means less counter space for everything else."*

Do you know what can look really beautiful on a kitchen counter? Baking ingredients! As long as you set up a station and give these items a purpose. For instance . . . decanting your ingredients in glass canisters that match the aesthetic of your space or even adding something fun into the mix, like cookbooks arranged in rainbow order.

3 *"People know that I like collecting coffee mugs. So now for every holiday, I get a bunch of mismatched mugs. I want my cabinets to look sleek and organized, but it's hard with so many sizes, shapes, and colors."*

In this case, just because a mug is a kitchen item doesn't mean it needs to live in the kitchen. If it's a sentimental item, it can be stored elsewhere—don't let it take up your valuable real estate. Joanna even recommends using mugs to store pencils on a desk!

4 *"A lot of my kitchen storage space is taken up by appliances and tools I only use occasionally. But there doesn't seem to be a more logical place to keep those things—and when I need them, I need them."*

If "occasionally" means every few months, your appliances can live elsewhere. For instance . . . maybe stored in a bin on the floor of your pantry. You might also want to think about downsizing some of your appliances. Even the bulkiest items have a sleeker, slimmer alternative.

"Every single drawer in my kitchen feels like a junk drawer. Seriously."

That usually means that you don't need all the items in your kitchen. Which is actually great news! It allows you to start fresh and come up with a new system that works for you.

THE FUNDAMENTALS CHECKLIST FOR ANY KITCHEN

Need to have:

- Storage system for plates, glasses, and cutlery
- Easy access and smart storage for pots and pans
- Organized system for cooking utensils
- Proper homes for appliances and leftovers containers
- Storage for infrequently used cooking and baking items

Nice to have:

- Pretty and functional stations (e.g., for coffee and tea; breakfast; candy!)
- Dedicated space for entertaining items
- Next-to-stove storage for spices and oils
- Command station to manage household schedules
- Full-time, on-demand chef who knows every single recipe in existence by heart

EARLY RISER

Do you live with someone who likes to get up well before dawn to make sure you have a freshly baked scone, still warm from the oven and waiting on a plate for you when you wander into the kitchen for breakfast? We don't either, but it sure sounds nice.

For all the bakers out there, we hear that storing the variously shaped stuff you need can be harder than actually making those fresh scones before dawn, not that we would know. This client lives in an apartment with somewhat limited cabinet space and very little drawer storage beneath the countertops. She wanted an easy way to maintain the tools she uses for baking, from small ramekins to giant mixing bowls to the pretty cake stand she uses to display her results. Because her cabinets are fairly tall, we gave her risers to make use of the vertical space, and four-sort dividers (which have truly countless uses for nearly every room of the house) to keep the baking sheets and other flat items in line.

Now she just needs to invite us back for breakfast.

RISE AND SHINE

A setup like this can help you feel like you've got it together to face whatever the day is going to throw at you. This client has beautiful glassware, mugs, and plates but needed everything to go in one cabinet. We gave her clear risers so the shelves would still feel light and open, and doubled her storage space in the process. (We like to refer to risers as *bunk beds for inanimate objects* for obvious reasons.) Now the sets are easy to see and to access, and we adjusted the shelves so her infrequently used—but tall—items can stay on the top shelf. If you're not a fan of clear acrylic, there is also a wire option.

JUST APPLY YOURSELF

There are people in this world who like to keep their appliances out in the open, hogging the countertop, collecting dust, and possibly making them feel guilty every time they walk into the kitchen just to be reminded how infrequently they cook. And then there are the rest of us. We get it—sometimes appliances need to live on the counter because that's the only available space. But if you have the choice, we strongly encourage you to keep appliances that aren't used on the regular out of sight.

Unless you need the arm workout—and in which case, maybe consider weights?—ideally you should store heavy appliances in the cabinets beneath your counters, as we have done here; in a perfect world, you've even got an electrical outlet somewhere nearby. We adjusted these shelves to allow a tall blender and standing mixer to live on top; the clear bins in the space below are perfect for attachments and small appliances. (If you don't have this much height in your bottom cabinets, you can put the tall, heavy items on risers with attachments beneath; lighter appliances like the coffee grinder and miniprocessor can then go into upper cabinets.)

ALISON ROMAN
THE COOK'S ATELIER
ABRAMS
snacking cakes
STELLA PARKS
JOANNA GAINES
Salad for President
ABRAMS
JOANNE CHANG
Pastry Love
modern comfort food
barefoot contessa cookbook
LAUNDRY COOKBOOK
THOMAS KELLER
Convection Fan

SOLVING THE PUZZLE

Like a Rubik's cube, an undercounter cabinet can be approached in any number of ways. When it comes to storing pots and pans, though, just as with a Rubik's cube, there's really only one final answer: a wire cookware organizer.

Yes, we could have chosen to nest the skillets on top of each other. But here's why we didn't:

- a teeter-tottering stack of cookware not only looks awful but makes access harder
- nesting just means the client is inviting moisture + bacteria growth (terrifying) unless everything has been put away bone dry
- the unwieldy handles

We opted for the divider to separate both pans and lids by size, with handles facing out and at the ready when needed. We can't tell our client exactly what to cook in those skillets (why so many sizes?!?), but we can guarantee that they'll have no trouble keeping this system in place.

PUT A LID ON IT. (OR NOT.)

By now we have firmly established to our loved ones, fans, and curious bystanders alike that we have a unique mind meld that binds us together. We understand each other's preferences, idiosyncrasies, and worldviews. When confronted with a problem, we often independently come to the same solution. Our relationship is truly a beautiful thing, shifting from friendship to business and back to friendship again, all in the space of a normal morning. We wake up every day thanking our mutual friend, Leah, who set us up on a blind lunch date that changed everything.

But if we ever break up (we won't!), it's going to be because of lids. Because on the issue of lids, we do not, and possibly never will, see eye to eye. We once had a very intense fight over food storage, and we just had to agree to disagree.

In short,

- Clea believes that lids and containers should be stored separately (Exhibit A), because it's a better use of space and everything can be put away without being completely dry.
- Joanna believes that lids and containers should be stored together (Exhibit B), so you can keep a whole set together without having to search for a match later.
- Both systems work (we admit to each other, grudgingly). So if you have a preference and must take sides, it's better to just keep that information to yourself.

EXHIBIT A

EXHIBIT B

Five Kitchen Items SUMNER WANTS TO TALK TO YOU ABOUT

If you keep any of the following items in your kitchen (and add the eight can openers you own to the list!), Sumner wants to *see into your soul and wonder why that is*.

1 **Potato Masher:** Certainly, there's a TikTok hack for something else you can use. You can't even put them in a drawer—or else the drawer won't close. How often are you hand mashing potatoes, realistically? You're not. You are not. We live in an automated world; just use your hand mixer.

2 **XL Roasting Pan:** I get that you put it on your wedding registry, but this is a holiday item. Who's out here basting and roasting turkeys twelve months out of the year? No one I know. Store it with your other holiday items and bring it out at the appointed time. It does not need to take up real estate the size of a Manhattan studio in your kitchen.

3 **Take-Out Utensils:** What are you stockpiling them for? You need to be saying, "No, I don't need utensils" when you place an order. Do that self-improvement work in your life.

4 **Meat Thermometers:** People either have zero or ten. This is true for any house I have ever been in. I'm waiting to meet the person who has one.

5 **Grilling Tools:** Those are outdoor items; they are not kitchen items. They are too large and in charge to live in a kitchen. They are scaled as an item that lives outdoors and is used by Paul Bunyan. I get the human impulse to think "this is cooking," but it's a different type of cooking.

TOP DRAWER

Have you ever opened a drawer in your kitchen, took one look inside, and thought, *OMG, no thank you, and now I need a nap or a drink to recover from what I just saw?* This does not regularly happen to us; otherwise, how could we possibly help you? But it *does* happen.

Ah, the junk drawer. Maybe it holds pens and paper clips; maybe it holds spatulas and measuring spoons. Most kitchens have one (or five) and most people think it's just an inconvenience that needs to be worked around. A necessary evil that must be endured as a means to an end, like screaming preteens at a Harry Styles concert.

Wrong! Here, we humbly submit the four-step system to tackle any kind of drawer:

1 Empty the drawer. We mean it—take everything out. Even stuff you know you want to keep. Once it's empty, take a few minutes to wipe it clean of random crumbs, lint, all of it.

2 Toss or donate what you don't want, use, or need, and then clear a big space (the countertop really comes in handy here) to

group the things you are keeping into categories, clocking any duplicates. (If you have, say, five different bottle openers, you already know what to do.)

3 Measure the drawer, from the inside edges, making a note of width, length, and height.

4 Find the insert system that works for you and your space.

KITCHEN

A few suggestions:

- Arrange items according to frequency of use.
- Try multiple small inserts—which can be arranged with more flexibility—rather than one giant one.
- Play around with configurations until you find the right combination (here's another Rubik's cube).
- Buy more inserts than you need (and return what you don't use)! Chances are you won't get it right the first time (and that's okay).
- Try spring-loaded expandable inserts if individual inserts don't work.
- Use museum gel—removable, reusable, and nontoxic—underneath your dividers to keep them in place.
- Embrace the trial and error.
- HAVE FUN. THIS IS FUN.

TASTE MASTERS

When we meet with a new client, one of the first things we ask about is what we call the "fussy factor." There are a lot of ways to measure your fussy factor, but one of the quickest is to know how you feel about decanting. We're not talking about wine. We're talking about coming home from the grocery store and pouring the thing you bought—which likely came in an oddly shaped or unattractive container—into another container that both matches and perfectly fits your space. Some people love to decant, and some don't.

We're not going to lie: We love a canister wall. This clever, shallow undercabinet shelf was the perfect solution for a high-fussy-factor client who thought decanting spices was her idea of a good time.

Which . . . same. (We even gave her a little ROYGBIV over the stove for an extra bit of magic.) Spices displayed like this both look like an art installation and couldn't be simpler to use; the clear panels let you see when you're running out, and everything is within easy reach. You could even DIY a shelf like this if your kitchen can accommodate it.

If decanting is not your thing, a simple turntable with spices and other cooking essentials works beautifully, either in a cabinet or out on the counter (if you must). We love a two-tier turntable for spices, which fits nicely beneath plates in a small kitchen. This client prefers to sort her spices in broad categories, but we've had requests for organizing spices by color, in alphabetical order—even into groups of sweet, savory, and salty. Just about any system works, as long as it's *your* system, tailored to the unique workings of your unique, beautiful brain.

GRAND AND CENTRAL

Whether your household is big or small, loud or quiet, organized or . . . less organized, you probably have a kitchen command station. You may not call it that, or even know it's there. But we all have a place where we keep track of life, wrangle important things that come in and out (including our kids), and generally keep our heads on straight.

The most important rule of thumb in maintaining a kitchen command station is that everything should at least tangentially involve every member of the household. In other words, this is not the spot for tax returns, or a Pokémon card collection—this area is about group functioning.

And a household command station doesn't have to be a computer on a desk. You just need something centrally located that everyone can access (and if you're short on space, you could even use a rolling cart). This client had an empty wall along one side of her kitchen that we outfitted with the family calendar (all hail the dry eraser), slots for outgoing mail, hooks for keys and other easy-to-misplace items, and a bulletin board for invitations and other little reminders. The whole space has a community bulletin board vibe: friendly, informational, and easy to modify and maintain.

SUNDAY
MONDAY
DAY
WEDNESDAY
THURSDAY
FRIDAY
SATURDAY
MAY
3 SCHOOL MUSICAL 6:30
6 SOCCER 12:00
8 DENTIST 9:30
14 FAMILY PHOTOS 3:00
18 LIBBY'S BIRTHDAY!
20 SOCCER 2:30
23 HAIR APPT. 4:30
26 HS GRADUATION 7:00
28 FLIGHT TO FL 8:30
29 BEACH DAY!
inbox
outbox
mail
BROADWAY
Thank you

KITCHEN

sugar
VENUS
FLEUR
SMEG

HIT STATION

If you read the closet chapter (and *of course you did*), you know how we feel about stations. But what you don't know yet is how we feel about stations in the kitchen. It's a whole other level.

What defines a great kitchen station? It's a highly edited space dedicated to one particular interest or activity that holds everything you need to enjoy said interest or activity. If something is part of a station, it has a clear (no pun intended) purpose, and so can live on the counter without being an eyesore.

Given the pace of our lives, we have a particular weak spot for a coffee station. It's really the MVP of the house every single day. Here, we set up everything needed for coffee or tea in a flash, from mugs to pods to the electric kettle, conveniently located next to an outlet. Extra mugs and backstock are in the cabinets above. There are any number of things that can be "stationed," and only you know what's best for your kitchen, but here are some suggestions: breakfast station; pet station; healthy snack station; baking station; dishwashing station . . . depending on your household, the list goes on and on.

WELL, THERE YOU GO

One client wanted a wellness station in her kitchen, filled with everything the members of her family needed for healthy drinks, from smoothies to coffee (yes, coffee = wellness) to water bottles. Clear bins that are both narrow and deep were the answer (see photo, page 199), both for the shelves (for ease of grabbing) and the drawers (for ease of sorting and storing).

While we're on the subject of wellness, let's take a moment to talk about water bottles. We have become a water bottle nation, and hopefully Mother Nature thanks us a little bit every day when we reach for a reusable bottle rather than a plastic disposable one.

BUT. We can't tell you the number of kitchens we've seen where our clients are nearly drowning in an ocean of water bottles they've collected from corporate events, charity runs, school fundraisers, you name it. *PSA:* If you are not using that water bottle, donate it! Or, if you must keep it for sentimental reasons (as a reminder that some long-ago version of you once ran a 5K), put it in sentimental storage. Your kitchen drawers and cabinets are too crucial for daily living to be crammed full of stuff you never use.*

*This also goes for commemorative mugs, insulated coffee cups, and those plastic glasses that come with overpriced drinks at professional sporting events (we beg you to stop collecting these).

LOW-BAR LIFESTYLE LONG-TERM GOALS

- Get an Instant Pot or air fryer. They take up quite a bit of real estate but they do multiple things. One large appliance that replaces multiple smaller ones . . . we'll take it! They are putting in the extra work and we respect that.

- Adjusting your shelves can feel like a gym workout. Go the easy route and add a riser instead.

- Store fruit in chic wire baskets on your countertop (preferably in rainbow order) so your kitchen looks like a farmers' market and you make healthier choices.

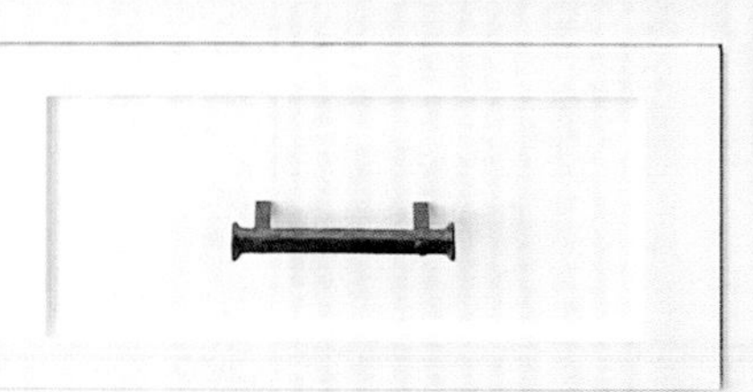

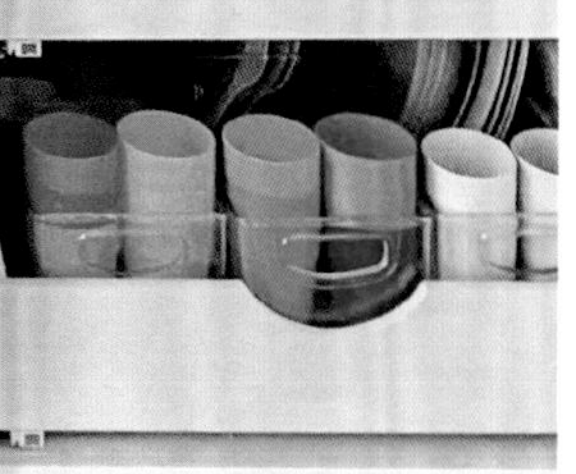

PANTRY & FRIDGE

DIFFICULTY LEVEL: ★★★★★★★★☆

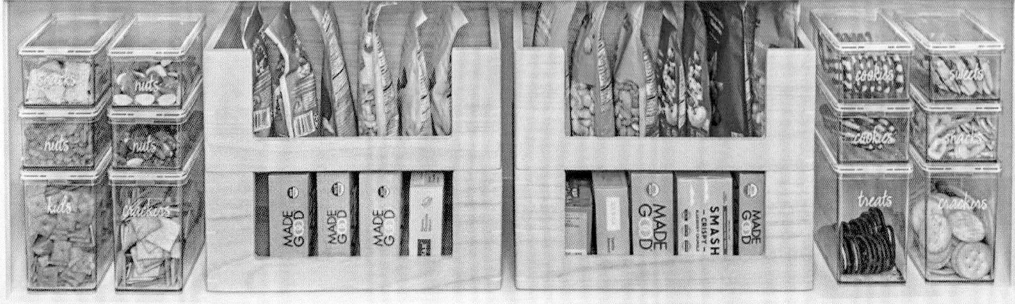

The problem with maintaining a pantry is that perfect organization is, by its nature, a fleeting thing. Trying to keep this crucial space in line is like trying to catch a snowflake. For a split second you hold it in your hand, and it's nearly miraculous in its perfection. And then it's gone. You catch another one, and it happens again. And again. And again.

If you live in a busy household, the problem may be your family. You can't blame them for needing to eat. But let's just say they are far from innocent. As soon as your pantry is organized, somebody goes to the grocery store, in an attempt to be "helpful," and unloads the newly purchased provisions in a way that would seem to make sense to . . . helpful people, but that completely ignores the system you so carefully set up. Not to mention violates all your sensibilities when it comes to the marriage of function and form.

We have seen our fair share of pantries. Pantries that are rooms as big as studio apartments, with rolling ladders for easy access to every single shelf, and pantries that are one small cabinet next to the stove, with shelves that are too high to reach. In other words: If you have food, you have a pantry, no matter its size or location. And if you have a pantry, you have a problem.

But don't worry! As women who love little moments of perfection, we know exactly what it's like to hold a snowflake and then feel the sinking disappointment as it disappears. And as professional organizers, we also know how to keep your organized pantry from doing the same thing.

FIVE MESSY PANTRY AND FRIDGE EXCUSES, DEBUNKED

1 *"My pantry is full of boxes and bags that are half full. I don't like to decant, and they take up a lot of space. But I also don't want to throw anything out."*

Will you eat all this food before it expires? If something is half full and it's been sitting in your pantry for a while, chances are it will continue to sit there ignored. To cut down on wasted food and wasted space, always check the current state of affairs before you go grocery shopping. What are people eating the most? What has been pushed deep into a corner? Let your past behavior be your future guide.

2 *"All I have for food storage is a small group of three shelves in my upper cabinets. I don't have space for much, and the shelves are so deep that I can't even see half of what I have."*

Clear bins act as makeshift drawers in this situation. You can pull one down and avoid having to search for things on your tiptoes. Turntables, stackable canisters, and tiered shelving are your other best friends here. All of these products help create more visibility and accessibility in hard-to-reach spaces.

3 *"Whenever my kids want a snack, they head to the pantry, open a bag or box, take a handful, and leave without closing the container. Sometimes they eat what's left and leave the empty container! I don't know if this is a pantry problem or a parenting problem."*

Kids love doing this! It's one of their greatest talents. We can assure you that you aren't a horrible parent, and that it's not you, it's definitely your pantry. And your kids . . . but can you blame them?!

Most packaging these days isn't designed with closure or user-friendliness in mind. You can't fix what's already broken, except in this case . . . you can. Just transfer everything to clear canisters. Popping the lid off and then back on is a whole lot easier to manage.

4 *"My refrigerator is like a sad, dark cave, full of mysterious objects that nobody wants to claim. The contents change so often, though, that I can't come up with an organizing system that works."*

ZONES!! YOU NEED ZONES!! And containers and labels to identify those zones!! Go with general categories rather than specific ones. Deli vs. Cheese—because Deli can also account for meats when needed. The systems you put in place should be able to flex over time.

5 *"I'm willing to do the work to decant dry goods into canisters, and I love the way it looks. But I'm never sure how to deal with that last little bit of food in the bottom when it's time to refill. It seems sort of gross to just add new stuff on top."*

Shake it . . . shake it real good. And then count it as your cardio for the day!

THE FUNDAMENTALS CHECKLIST FOR ANY PANTRY AND FRIDGE

Need to have:

- Adequate storage on shelves or in bins for all nonperishables
- Dedicated zones in fridge and freezer for like items
- Easy access to foods you eat every day

Nice to have:

- Turntables for bottles, jars, and cans
- Clear canisters to decant (if you plan to maintain it)
- Space for backstock storage
- Drawers or bins dedicated to grab-and-go snacks
- Containers that beep when the food inside is about to expire (surely the technology is there?)

BEST IN SHOW

Admit it: There is something so beautiful, so inspiring, so perfect about this pantry that somebody ought to turn this photo into wallpaper *(paging Joanna!)*. The clearly labeled canisters are just right for the space and separated into food types; the cans are grouped for easy access, on what we like to call "stadium seating" shelving; and turntables keep cooking ingredients such as sauces and oils always at the ready.

But here's what you don't see: how hard this kind of pantry is to maintain. It's not for everyone! Don't get us wrong: We *love* clients who are up to this challenge, and this client made it clear from the beginning that they were all in. They like the look, and they are willing to do the work.

pine nuts
dried chickpeas
split green peas
black beans
large lima beans
dried porcini mushrooms
cranberry beans
cannellini beans
red lentils
sprouted lentils
green lentils
black lentils
great white beans
casulet beans
short grain brown rice
farro
rice
risotto rice
polenta
couscous
red bulgur
freekhe
jasmine rice
sushi rice
pearled couscous
israeli couscous
EDEN ORGANIC GARBANZO
MUIR GLEN ORGANIC PETITE DICED
EDEN ORGANIC GARBANZO BEANS
PALMINI
LASAGNA
LINGUINE
365 ORGANIC Coconut
Organic Coconut Milk
ALBACORE
REFRIED BEANS
field DAY organic Garbanzo BEANS
WESTBRAE NATURAL
ORGANIC LENTIL BEANS

If a pantry like this is your goal, first you have to be honest, look deep into your organizing soul, and ask yourself a few questions:

1. Am I really going to want to decant all of these dry goods when they come home from the store?
2. Are the members of my household going to be on board, or is all the work going to fall to me? And, if so, am I okay with that?
3. Do I have food that I consume often enough that it merits using canister space? *(Looking at you, goji berries!)*
4. Similarly, do I really use all of the foods I'm tempted to buy and put in a canister?

If the answer to all the above questions is a resounding *yes*, and you have space for a canister system, we applaud you. If you answered *no* to any of the above, we recommend you hit Pause for a minute before you dive in. We've said it before, but it bears repeating: With any organizing system, there is no one-size-fits-all answer. The first—and most important—consideration is **what's the right system for YOU?**

PANTRY LANGUAGE

Here's Clea's pantry. Rainbow on full display. The first thing you might notice is that she doesn't decant everything—she only decants what makes sense for her family. The food she keeps in its original packaging goes into bins, organized by color (it's not unusual to hear one of her kids say, "Mom, we're running out of yellow snacks!"), and turntables keep ingredients always in reach.

When Clea began to set up her pantry, one thing that was immediately obvious was all the negative space on the floor.

PREMIUM
pasta
dinner
CLUB minis
snacks
cereal
pantry
pantry
pantry

Any sensible person knows that the floor and food can actually mix—within reason. You're probably not going to want to keep a wire basket of, say, potatoes, on the floor. But items in packaging (snacks in bags, bottles and cans) may be stored on the floor, so they're out of the way but still easy to find when they are needed to refill the canisters and bins on the shelves above. Bonus: This is a painless way to put the kids to work when inventory is low. So instead of calling Clea to refill the yellow snacks, her kids can do it themselves. They get a feeling of responsibility, she gets a little more time to herself (JK, time to herself doesn't exist).

ASPIRATIONAL TRAIL MIX

So what's with this canister array? Our client had a very specific request: Make healthy foods visible. Naturally, we created a full-service trail mix station, so when they feel like a snack, they reach for pepitas and banana chips instead of the s'mores makings that are winking at them from the Very Very High Shelf above. (We don't have the scientific data to prove this, but anecdotal evidence suggests that *healthy and convenient* prevails over *unhealthy and inconvenient* in nine out of ten matchups.) Once healthy snacks are part of a system, they feel intentional, and leaning into that system to maintain it will make you happy. Even when you are hungry and tempted to reach for the marshmallows.

(Fun fact: This was not our first extremely specific food station rodeo. Over the years, for various clients, we have created stations for smoothies, oatmeal, pasta night, taco night, and sushi night. If you organize a station around something that's special to the household, everyone gets excited, and keeping the station organized feels less like work and more like fun.)

PANTRY PARALYSIS PREVENTION

More than any other space in your house, your pantry requires organizing tools that can make or break the space. Maintaining it is a choose-your-own-adventure process that is one part **utility**, one part **household habits**, and one part **aesthetics**. Pantry paralysis sets in when you set up a system that doesn't take into account those three factors.

If your system is falling apart, take a minute to do a bit of organizing therapy—i.e., ask yourself who you are as a human being. While that may sound humongous and heavy (after all, this isn't Philosophy 101, it's just your pantry), know that the answer to the question will make the following steps that much easier.

After you've taken an honest look at yourself, take an honest look at your space and keep these questions in mind:

- How big is it?
- Does it have any odd elements, like tricky corners?
- How many shelves do you have?
- What are your shelves made of? How much weight can they hold, and, if they are wire, how will you prevent items from falling through?
- Regarding bins, do you want clear, wooden, wire, metal?
- How much backstock do you want and where does it go?

After we worked with the client to answer all of the above, we set to work to create this beauty. We employed a mix of containers—tall plastic canisters, round glass canisters, decorative woven bins, clear plastic bins, and turntables. For concealed storage, we kept everything at eye level or lower; generally, concealed storage overhead becomes a giant wasteland of stuff you've completely forgotten about. And most excitingly, a sweet snack station in the back creates a beautiful focal point for the whole pantry (and focal points are excellent for maintenance, because you will always want to keep that area looking nice).

crackers
baking
bakery

CAN I DATE YOU?

Often when we post a photo of beautifully decanted food on our Instagram, we imagine a silent scream goes out across the land, and it sounds something like this: But *what about cooking instructions and expiration dates??????????????*

Oh, friends, have a little faith. It may look—sometimes—like we are fanatical, and inflexible, and good at organizing and nothing else. We will proudly own all those things. But we do live in the real world, where people may not remember (or want to Google) how long it takes to boil penne, or when that beautiful canister of pasta may actually turn into fossilized rocks no longer safe for human consumption.

Here's an easy hack: Let your canister work a little harder for you. If you want to save the cooking instructions, just tape them to the canister; the bottom works, but if you attach them to the lid, you can see them easily when you open the canister to cook. Ditto expiration dates; here we used a label maker, but you can also write on the canister with a washable paint pen. Extra points if you have legible handwriting. And if you don't, Clea is more than happy to stop by.

Penne Rigate no. 41
Suggestion
for perfect cooking
Use 6 quarts of water per 1 lb of pasta
Bring water to a boil. Add salt to taste.
Add pasta to boiling water.
Stir from time to time.

7/24

BEFORE

DRAWERS + DOOR = YIKES

As professional organizers with clients all over the place who live in all manner of houses and apartments, we've seen a lot of scary stuff. As moms with kids, we've seen a lot of scary stuff. And Clea loves *Dateline*! She's *really* seen some scary stuff. But there is nothing that scares us more than hidden drawers. Drawers behind doors are what nightmares are made of when you are people like us.

It's kind of like that lesson you learn in high school chemistry: There are certain harmless substances that, when combined, nevertheless form a toxic gas. It's the same when you combine drawers and doors. They are both harmless (extremely useful, even), but when combined, can result in a hidden, sloppy, toxic mess that requires a road map to escape.

This family of five had plenty of space but needed a road map they could consistently follow to keep the drawer + door combination from becoming a horror show.

DRAWERS + DOOR: THE SOLUTION

First things first: We nixed the shelf that was bowed in the middle and reconfigured the remaining two. No more wrestling with cleaning supplies (which honestly shouldn't live with food anyway, unless you have no choice) on the neglected top shelf. Now that space has enough height to accommodate tall canisters filled with essentials; on the shelf below, extralarge turntables make the most of the shelf, holding jars and cans. With dedicated zones for food types, these shelves will be easy for the adults in the house to maintain.

But it's the drawers that steal the show here. While this family already had the luxury of big drawers, and they were already using bins to separate items, there was room for improvement, both literally and figuratively. Now snacks are divided into adult and kid drawers (although we certainly know adults who eat Nutella and animal crackers, not naming names), with the kids' snack drawers in the lower compartments. We gave them labels to separate sweet and savory, but your labeling system should be tailored to your family: You could label things by type of snack or by family member or even shape—whatever makes sense for you.

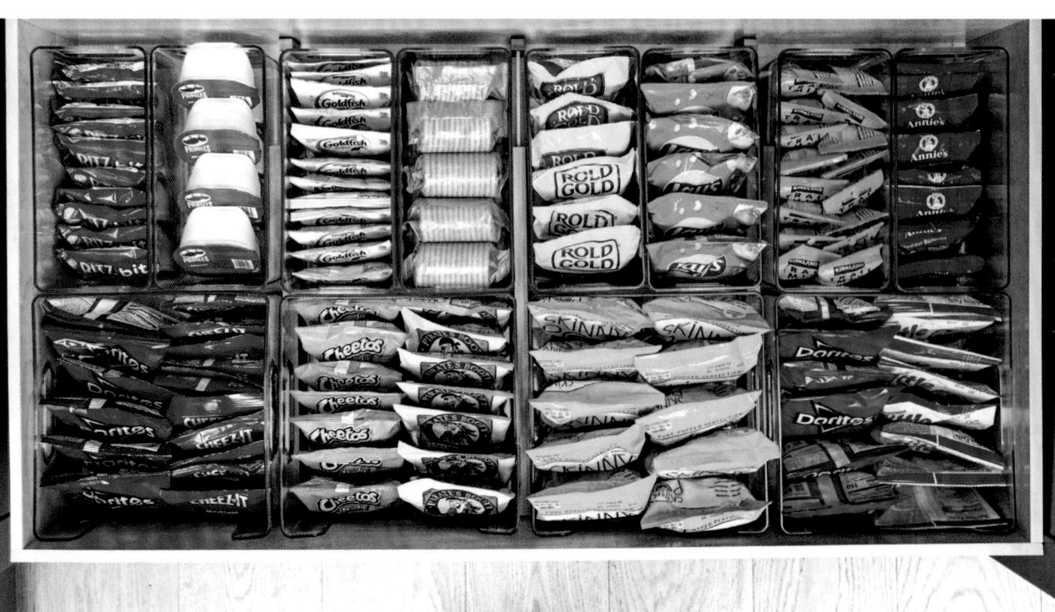

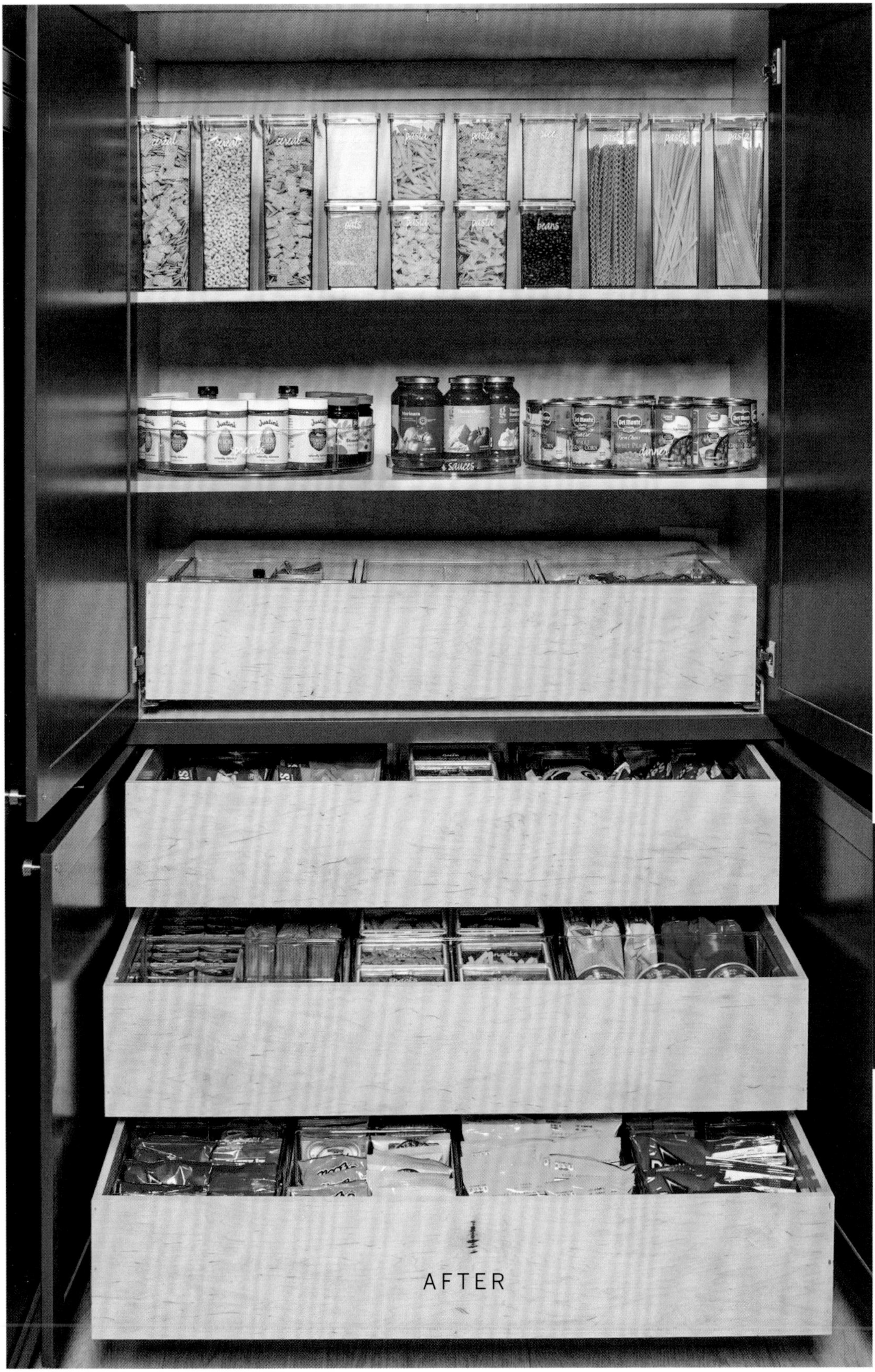

AFTER

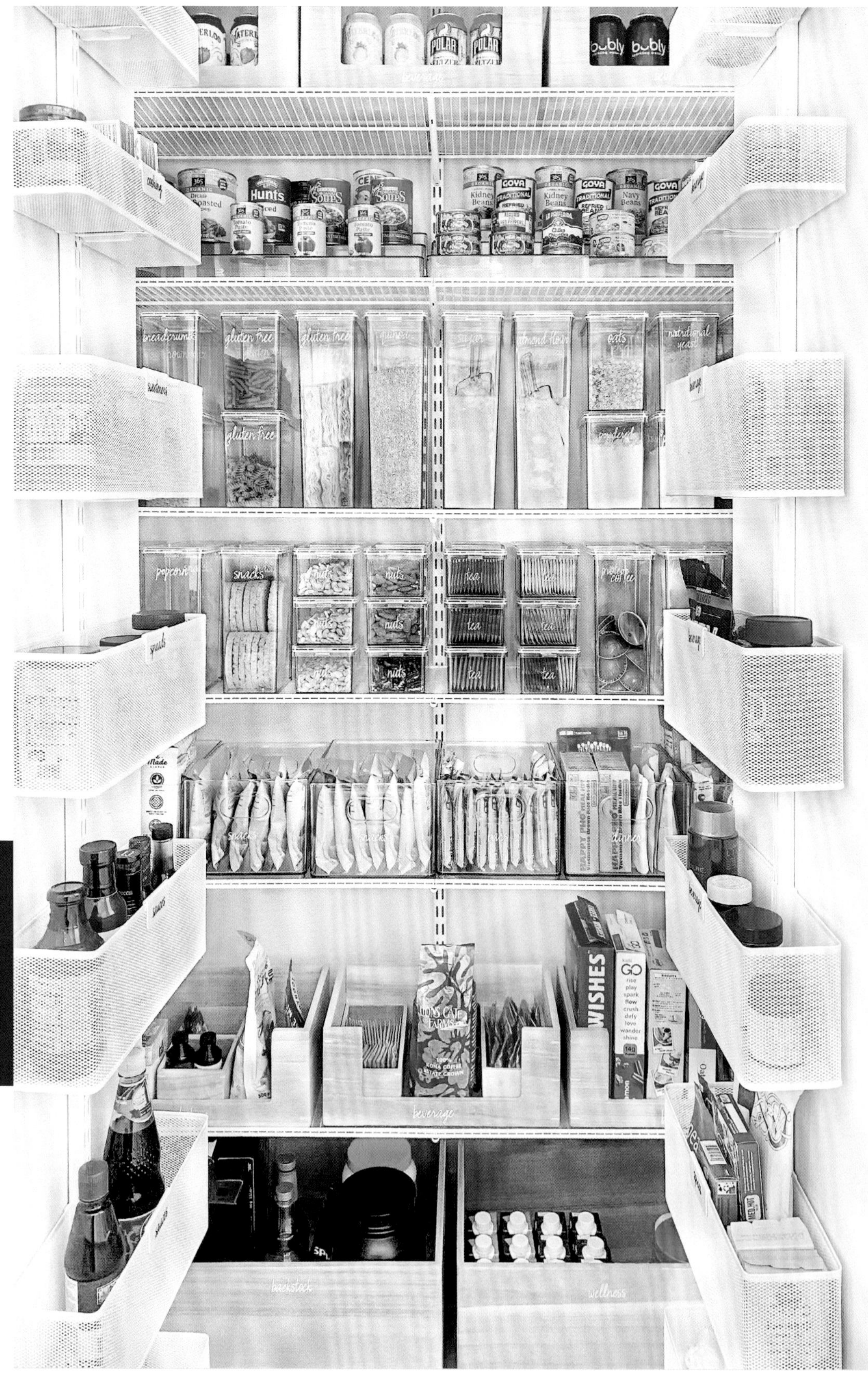
POLAR
SELTZER
bubly
Hunts
GOYA
TRADITIONAL
Kidney Beans
Navy Beans
breadcrumbs
gluten free
gluten free
quinoa
sugar
almond flour
oats
nutritional yeast
gluten free
powdered
popcorn
snacks
nuts
nuts
nuts
tea
tea
tea
protein coffee
snacks
snacks
WISHES
GO
rise
play
spark
flow
crush
defy
love
wander
shine
beverage
backstock
wellness

When you're organizing your own snack supply in a household with kids, ask yourself how the kids reach for things. Drawers are a no-brainer for little ones, but your snack system can evolve as your kids grow. Because the children in this household are young, it's going to take an adult to monitor the snack supply, ideally going through everything once a week or so and taking stock. But older kids are *all too eager* to notice and let the Tall Person Who Drives to the Store know when the Oreo bin is running on empty.

MIX AND MATCH

Ever heard that expression about how good things come in small packages? That's exactly how we feel about this pantry. When you're dealing with a relatively small space, you need to think outside the bin, and use your imagination to determine which products best fit where. Basically, throw out the rule book and make your own (armed with the lessons we've given you, OBVIOUSLY).

Here, we opted for mixed materials based on the client's space and lifestyle. Open-front bins hold quick-grab items in their original packaging, creating their own ministations that can almost slide out like drawers; clear bins hold individual snack servings; canisters hold everything from a rainbow of tea bags to baking ingredients. Storing cans on high shelves can be tricky (you can't always see what's in back), but tiered stadium seating keeps everything in sight. Finally, we made use of the negative space on the floor and door, where labels help keep everyone in the family on board with maintenance.

BEFORE

USE IT OR LOSE IT

The good news: This client already understood the basics. They had turntables for condiments, clear bins for produce and snacks, and food more or less organized into zones. But they weren't using all the space wisely (um, the empty shelf on the door), there were unholy marriages (pickles and wine?), and the squeezable kids' snacks lying loose on their sides just made us feel . . . sad.

AFTER

We didn't have to do much to get this busy refrigerator back in shape. A paint pen came in handy to label the drawers—yes, do try this at home—and we added additional bins (even within the drawers themselves), labeled where it made sense, to help everybody in the household know how and when to restock. We kept only the (unexpired!) condiments that the family uses and allowed the champagne that was previously living a lonely life in a cabinet to join the party. It did mean saying goodbye to the pickles. But that was a sacrifice we were all willing to make.

breakfast
fruit
fruit
fruit
fruit
produce
produce
deli
snacks

DECANTING ASMR . . .

. . . or why the sound these foods make while you pour them into that pretty canister may actually be good for your brain:

- Lentils
- Rice
- Jelly beans
- Chocolate chips
- Grape-Nuts
- Pasta
- Sprinkles
- Granulated sugar

LOW-BAR LIFESTYLE LONG-TERM GOALS

- When editing, take the opportunity to give your pantry and fridge shelves a much-needed wipe down. Cleaning and organizing are different things, but when you achieve them both at the same time, it's a bonus gold star.
- Bindication is real. If you can't manage canisters, just say yes to bins. You'll be much happier in the long run.
- Resist buying the family-size box of cereal when you know you don't have the space.

GARAGE

DIFFICULTY LEVEL: ★★★★★★★★★

Congratulations! You've made it through all the rooms of your house, and now spaces both large and small have been improved by your dedicated efforts . . . almost. There's just one more teeny-tiny thing: THE GARAGE.

You may have noticed that we've rated the garage a 9-gold-star accomplishment. And why is that, exactly? It's not because we assume you spend a lot of time in your garage, or that maintaining organization there is particularly difficult. It's just that we don't really *like* the garage. (You can say the same about the basement and the attic.) Remember, we have no hobbies. Which means that most garages are full of tools that we don't use, equipment for sports that we don't play, items necessary for landscaping and car care that we don't understand, and storage for random items that have nowhere else to live. Plus, unpleasant (but necessary) garbage and recycling bins.

Can we go back to the pantry?

Just kidding! (Sort of.) We do know that not everyone shares our biases, and that the garage is an important functional space in most homes. It's like an unappreciated part of your body. Like your ankle. Ankles absorb constant pressure, but you probably don't spend a lot of time thinking about your ankles. Until there's a problem, and then you feel pain with every step. The garage is the same. It's one area that tends to absorb all the pressure of the household in terms of bits and baubles that don't seem to go together or defy categorization. It's all too easy to throw things in the garage and forget about them until the day that you can't get to your car door because it's blocked by piles of random stuff. And then . . . feel the pain with every step.

Even though we are not crazy about the garage, we know it's a space that can make *you* crazy. And so, because we love you, we invite you to step into the garage. We promise it won't hurt a bit.

FIVE MESSY GARAGE EXCUSES, DEBUNKED

1 *"My garage is the dumping ground where we put everything we don't really know what to do with. There is no rhyme, reason, or order!"*

Same with most people! That's why we made the garage 9 stars. It's not fun having to sift through a mix of items that you know you need but don't necessarily want. Even if you rarely access them, these items should be accounted for. You need to put systems in place that are functional for your lifestyle. But first, you must see what you are working with. Remove everything, pare down, and group your categories. Ready, set, go . . .

2 *"With four kids who all do different sports, my garage is overflowing with balls and sticks and rackets and pads that are assorted shapes and sizes. I can't figure out a system to contain all these weird things."*

This is the worst. Thankfully, we passed on our lack of athletic ability to our children. No basketballs or other bulky items in sight! But we still help other people deal with them. The key is to get everything up off the ground and to designate zones by sport, then shape and size. The specialty storage options really shine here.

3 *"My partner is a car fanatic and loves to tinker in the garage. And he leaves his tools everywhere. It doesn't seem to bother him, but it drives me nuts."*

We're happy to report that you're not completely screwed! *(Hahahaha, sorry, we had to!)* If your partner is always in the middle of a project, they won't want to keep opening up drawers to put things away, just to get them right back out. Hang a magnetic pegboard and use wall storage instead. The path of least resistance always wins . . . but especially here.

4 *"I have a two-car garage, but once we have both cars in there, the space is very narrow. I can't figure out how to create storage that leaves space for cars and people to walk around."*

BUT IS IT a two-car garage?!! Some garages claim they are two-car garages, but that's true only if both cars are extremely small. One large car, one small car? Not a chance. This is your moment of reckoning: both cars, no storage, or one car, a decent amount of storage? Ponder on that and move forward accordingly.

5 *"I don't have a garage! So, I have no idea where to store all the typical 'garage' stuff I have that is too messy to keep in my apartment."*

Unfortunately, this simply means you can't own a lot of "garage" stuff. Since you don't have a garage and your home can't become your garage, where's the happy medium? Giving yourself a "garage" bin and holding yourself accountable when you start exceeding that space. Zones, y'all!

THE FUNDAMENTALS CHECKLIST FOR ANY GARAGE

Need to have:

- Solid shelving to hold heavy tools or equipment
- Bins with lids for anything that needs to stay clean
- Wall-mounted units to hang anything that has a stick
- Closed containers for anything that has an odor (like garbage)

Nice to have:

- Bins on wheels to store items that need to be loaded into the car
- Open shelving for shoe storage
- Clear bins to store holiday décor or off-season entertaining needs
- Peg board or drawers for tools
- Kids who choose activities that don't require bulky equipment (i.e., cheerleading, musical theater, playing the flute)

CLEAR VISION

If you've got a bunch of unrelated items in a garage—and who doesn't?—the easiest way to unify the space is with clear bins. Even if they are of different sizes and full of wildly disparate stuff, as they are here (golf balls + blankets + spray paint!), clear bins make everything appear intentional and tidy. In this space, as with many, the best system for our client was shelving; once the cars are inside, most garages don't have enough clearance from car to wall to allow for doors that open.

GUAVA FAMILY
HALO
christmas
christmas
christmas
christmas
ornaments
ornaments
ornaments
ornaments
halloween
halloween
baby
baby

UNDECK THE HALLS

Group poll . . . who thinks we should be able to leave our holiday decorations up all year round?! Us too!! But since this world is full of Scrooges, here are tips to keep them protected and easier to unpack when the time comes:

- Take photos of the decorated rooms before you start packing up to use as a reference for next year. It will simplify the unpacking process when you can visually see what you have and where it needs to go.

- Edit as you go. Fight the urge to shove everything back into storage bins without editing first. It's a waste of space and energy to pack and then unpack items that shouldn't be there in the first place. Keep a few garbage bags nearby to toss or donate the items that have reached their expiration date.

- Store in good condition. If something is broken, fix it or toss it. If something is dirty, clean it. It takes more effort to resurrect an item after it's been in storage, so just take care of it now so life is easier later.

- **Label E-V-E-R-Y-T-H-I-N-G.** Just because you access these items once a year doesn't mean you should skip labeling. In fact, it's even more of a reason to label because you're even more likely to forget.

If you opt for an artificial tree and have vertical space, use a protective tree bag and store it all in one piece, lights included. Another option is wrapping and labeling each part, then storing it in a bin.

GRAY MATTERS

Behold the quiet beauty of Joanna's garage. It will surprise no one to learn that it didn't look like this when she bought her house; apparently, "before" photos of the garage do exist somewhere in the world, but Joanna has made sure that no one will ever see them.

And the "after" is so satisfying, it hardly matters where she started. She chose gray for the drawer fronts and added a gray insert to the lidded bins to make the labels easier to read (plus it just looks really good). Because she is a paper person, Joanna likes to save documents and receipts, which she organizes by year and stores on the top shelves. The items that are more about straight utility live on the bottom shelves.

STICK 'EM UP

The secret sauce of organization is equal parts knowing what you have and where to put it all away. A pegboard can guarantee both, because it keeps everything clearly in view while providing a specific spot for each item. The tools on Joanna's garage pegboard could have been organized in all manner of ways, but since no one in her family uses them and they are more for show, a rainbow was necessary.

GET A GRIP

Have you ever heard us encourage someone to "shop the whole store"? It's advice we use fairly often. Despite how it sounds, we're not encouraging you to buy more. We're encouraging you to look beyond the obvious when you need an organizing solution.

Like how these gripped spice drawer inserts are the perfect solution for storing tools! Next time you head out to the store, try it. We promise you'll look at things in a different—and potentially more useful—light.

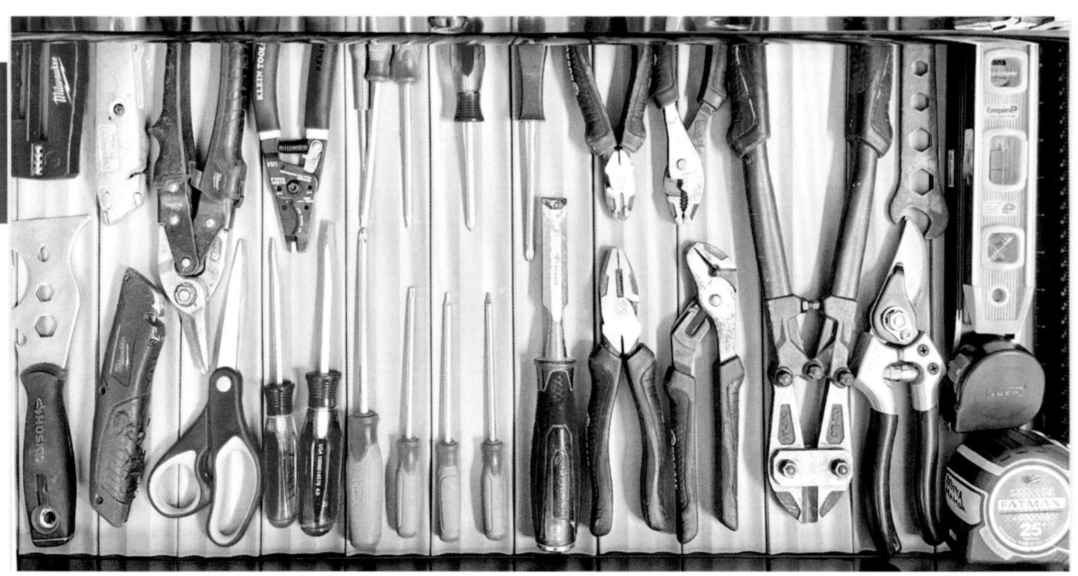

CRAFT SERVICES

Clea's kids are very clear on two things: One, that she loves them profoundly, in a way that she will never be able to properly express, and two, that they are not allowed to have messy craft supplies anywhere in the house. This is actually the only reason Clea can tolerate the garage: because it's the place that keeps messy paint, and anything with glitter, far, far away.

Which is not to say it shouldn't be organized appropriately. Or that stations can't be involved. Hence the messy craft station, with a kid-friendly turntable. Where the kids can go play and know that their mother will never, ever join them.

FOOT PATROL

"Where are my shoes?!?" How many times a week does someone in your house utter—or yell—that question? This client has a big, busy family, which meant lots of shoes and activities, and dirt tracked in the house whenever anybody came home. Because they have a garage with lots of available wall space, we created a modified shoe closet; now footwear comes off before it even makes it to the door. This system may not be ideal if your house has multiple entry points, but if most of your daily household foot traffic involves a trip through the garage, it could be perfect.

BEING GREEN

Maybe we don't know who you are or where you live, but it's safe to say that the recycling rules in your town are different from the ones in ours. Which is why, when we come to visit you, we are likely to recycle the wrong way: mixing cardboard with plastic because that's how it goes where we live, or not taking the labels off cans because we don't have to do that in our town. Proper recycling is important, but it's not simple. Make it easy on yourself, your family, and any out-of-town guests by having clearly delineated bins for the various methods of recycling where you live. It's a win for the planet and a win for your mental state.

HERE FOR CHEER

Every once in a while, we're confronted with an object that seems . . . unorganizable. Stubborn. Ill-fitting. Weirdly shaped and/or incapable of just getting in line. We were this close to adding "wreath" to that difficult list until we noticed this sliver of empty wall space in our client's garage [*cue angels singing*]. When you're maintaining your garage, don't forget about the negative space—especially when the end result can bring holiday cheer all year long.

ON A ROLL

Have you ever been in a sports equipment jungle? That's Joanna's term for a space where balls and bats and sticks and soccer balls and rackets and running shoes (tell us when to stop) have no clear home. So when you need something, you must go on a hunt, and inevitably you find yourself as lost and confused as if you were in the middle of the rain forest. Not that we would know, although we have seen *Jurassic Park*.

We know you need access to your stuff, and that you must quickly load up the car with whatever equipment is required for whatever sporty thing you're doing that day. For this client, we found the answer in rolling bins that separated bulky outdoor and sporting equipment. The labels are general enough that our client's family members don't have to think too hard when putting stuff away, but specific enough that folding chairs won't get mixed in with basketballs. Go team! Touchdown!

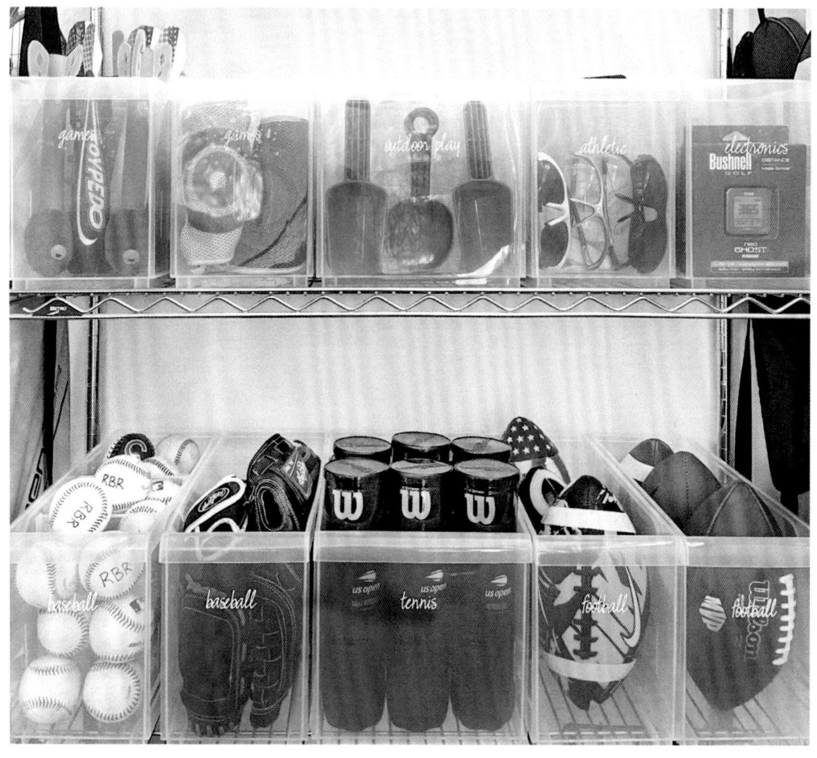

LOW-BAR LIFESTYLE LONG-TERM GOALS

- Stop dirt from sneaking into the house with a rubberized mat in the garage and a fabric rug that meets people as soon as they step inside.

- "Front" the items stored in clear bins. This means placing the prettier items in the front and the less attractive ones in the back. It's such a simple tweak that changes the entire look of a space.

- When in doubt, install a mount.

lights
lights

ornaments
ornaments

GIVE YOURSELF A GOLD STAR

VICTORY LAP

YOU DID IT!!! You have come a long way . . . time to collect all your gold stars!! If you've used the strategies in this book, the rooms of your house now feel reorganized, with systems refreshed and humming along nicely. But it's worth reminding yourself *why* you made the effort to "control the controllables," as we like to say. Your spaces are improved—and so is your headspace. Because maintenance is an act of self-care that saves you time, money, and sanity; it provides closure and calm when you part with possessions you no longer need or love; and it makes you feel good about yourself as you feel good about your home.

Which is not to say that your rooms are going to look like this forever. You still need to check in with each space on a regular basis. To determine how often, keep this simple formula in mind:

NUMBER OF PEOPLE WHO USE THE SPACE X FREQUENCY OF USE = HOW OFTEN THE SPACE NEEDS TO BE MAINTAINED

Please be kind to yourself if your maintenance starts to slip; after all, it probably means that you have a full, interesting life. Still, be extravigilant during these times, when your systems are liable to be challenged:

- Major life change (a move, a new family member)
- Children outgrowing toys and clothes
- Change of seasons
- Holidays

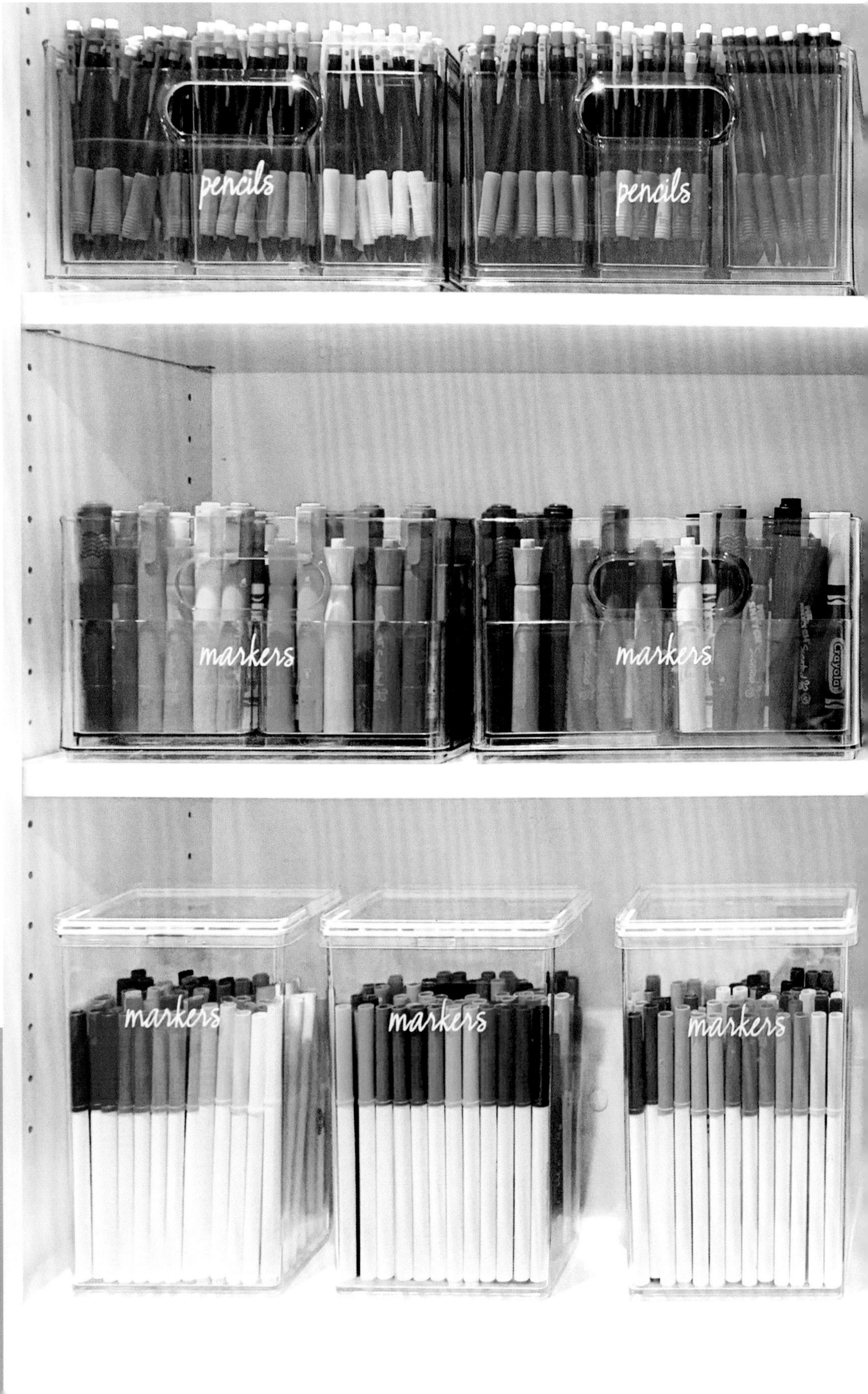
pencils
pencils
markers
markers
markers
markers
markers

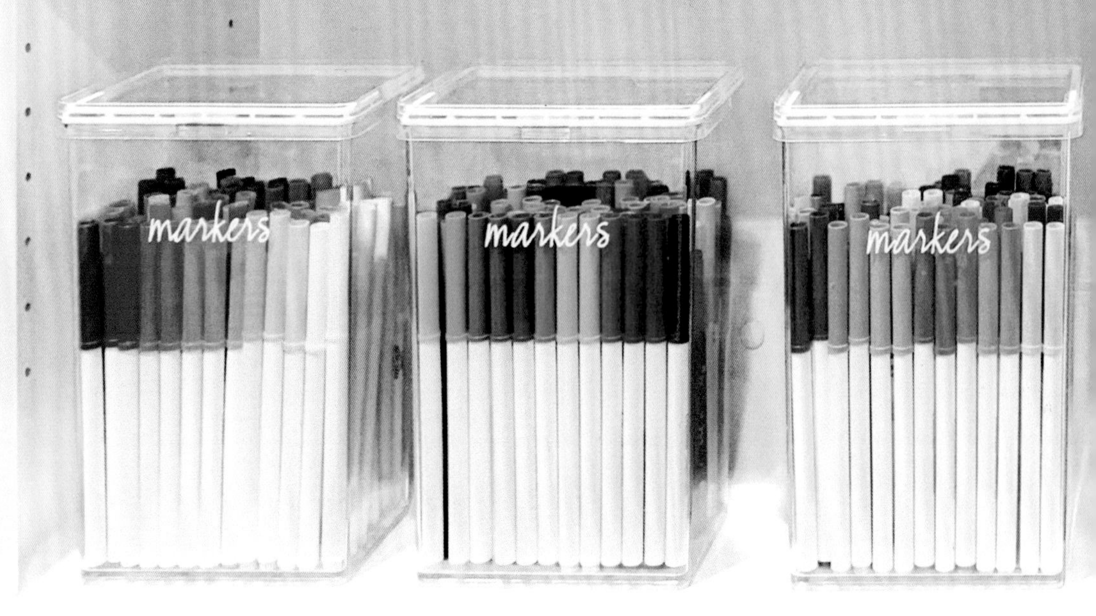

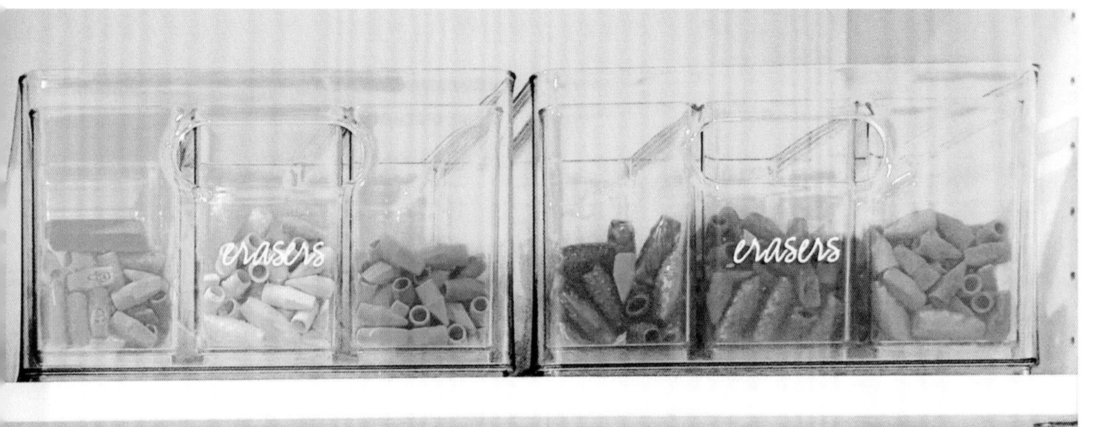
erasers
erasers

sharpies
sharpies

colored pencils
colored pencils
colored pencils

And look out for these signs that you need a refresh:

- Things are accumulating in piles.
- Drawers are not closing; items fall on your head when you open a cabinet (!).
- You find yourself searching for things you need.
- You find things migrating to places they don't belong.
- Your family members aren't following reasonable systems.

The good news is that there are small things you can do—five-minute tasks!—to feel like you are getting back on track. Room by room, here are some of our favorites:

THE ENTRY: Put away shoes.

LAUNDRY/UTILITY ROOM: Sort the laundry by family member (and if you have extra time, separate by category).

BATHROOM: Push toothpaste to top of tube (weirdly satisfying).

KIDS' ZONES: Gather outgrown toys for donation.

HOME OFFICE: Go through your mail (if a paper person) or email (if digital).

CLOSET: Take a pass through one category and make sure you are using and loving each item.

KITCHEN: Clear your countertops.

PANTRY AND FRIDGE: Check expiration dates on one category (canned goods, for instance).

GARAGE: Get things off the floor.

DON'T FORGET THE CART

We have sung the praises of the rolling cart several times, but it's worth repeating one more time: Never underestimate the transformative power of a cart on wheels. They just can't be beat in terms of organization and convenience. In a small room, they can be used as extra storage when space is tight. And in a large room, they can be moved around when needed and pushed aside when not. A moveable bar cart, for example, can travel from kitchen to living room to porch—to wherever the party is happening—and then kept in an underused space in the home until the next time it's needed.

KITCHEN
SESAME GINGER
DRESSING & MARINADE
AVOCADO OIL
8 FL OZ (236 mL)
KITCHEN
HONEY MUSTARD
DRESSING & MARINADE
AVOCADO OIL
8 FL OZ (236 mL)
PRIMAL KITCHEN
CILANTRO LIME
DRESSING & MARINADE
AVOCADO OIL
KITCHEN
RANCH
DRESSING & MARINADE
AVOCADO OIL
NO DAIRY
8 FL OZ (236 mL)

Finally, thank you for trusting us to help you on this journey. As a parting gift, we leave you with our favorite motivating affirmations. Focus on the one that speaks to you and cross out the rest:

- **Like working out, organizing is the gift that keeps giving;** if you form the habit, you can remind yourself of the benefit, even when you are dreading the task.
- **Maintenance is self-care,** just like treating yourself to your favorite cup of coffee, or a manicure, or whatever little reward works for you.
- **Drop the guilt! All lives get messy.** It's how you address the mess that matters.
- **Optimism will often save the day;** whatever type of organizer you are, you have the ability to stay organized. And you owe it to yourself.

Hippos
PICTIONARY

From 1-20
SECOND THOUGHTS

Thanks

Thank you, as always, to our incredible team at The Home Edit and Hello Sunshine for supporting us every step of the way. To our incredible publishing team at Clarkson Potter—Jenny Davis, Mia Johnson, Mark McCauslin, Kim Tyner, Aaron Wehner, and to Lindsay Edgecombe, our literary agent, and to Angelin Adams, our editor—for guiding us through not one, not two, but THREE books with such patience and brilliance. And to our lawyer, Matt Feil, for answering our calls and making sure we break zero laws.

An extra-special thank-you to Lauren Lagarde, Shaina Burrell, Courtney Cohen, and Kristin van Ogtrop for their super-human abilities in making this book come together. From creative and art direction to content and editing—this book would not have happened without you. And thank you to our readers, listeners, followers, and fans for making our dreams a reality. The Home Edit community wouldn't be the same without you and we are so glad you are here.

From Clea:
I'd like to thank John, Stella, and Sutton for their strength, bravery, and love during the hardest year of all of our lives. To my family (especially my mother!), friends (especially Joanna!), and team (literally all of you!)—your unwavering support means the world to me. I couldn't do anything without you.

From Joanna:
Nothing would be possible without the immense and consistent support from Jeremy, Miles, and Marlowe. Additionally, I must thank not only my family but also the entire THE team, for their incredible ideas, tenacity, and determination to complete this book. And, last—but most certainly not least—I want to thank the bravest warrior, most brilliant storyteller, and literally the world's best business partner and friend, Clea Shearer. Without you, none of this would exist.

INDEX

An Hachette UK Company
www.hachette.co.uk

First published in Great Britain in 2023 by Mitchell Beazley,
an imprint of Octopus Publishing Group Ltd
Carmelite House
50 Victoria Embankment
London EC4Y 0DZ
www.octopusbooks.co.uk

Photographic acknowledgements:
17, 116, 149, 170–71 ©John Shearer
2, 6, 18, 26, 36, 40, 48, 50, 57, 72, 74–75, 77, 82-3, 96-97, 114, 127, 128, 138, 140, 152–53, 164, 182, 183, 184, 187, 195, 212, 213, 237, 241, 242, 248. © Richard Bradley for Accenture Song
35 © Meagan Little Photography
108–9, 178–79, 196, 247 © 2023 Mary Craven Dawkins
167 © Mattie James
181 © Brittany Ambridge

ISBN 978-1-78472-906-6

A CIP catalogue record for this book is available from the British Library.

Printed in China

Designers: Mia Johnson and Jennifer K. Beal Davis

10 9 8 7 6 5 4 3 2 1